Soul
Angels

JENNY SMEDLEY

Soul Angels

HAY HOUSE

Australia • Canada • Hong Kong • India
South Africa • United Kingdom • United States

Previous Publications
by Jenny Smedley

Past Life Meditation CD

Past Life Angels

Souls Don't Lie

The Tree That Talked

How to Be Happy

Pets Have Souls Too

Angel Whispers

First published and distributed in the United Kingdom by:
Hay House UK Ltd, 292B Kensal Rd, London W10 5BE. Tel.: (44) 20 8962 1230;
Fax: (44) 20 8962 1239. www.hayhouse.co.uk

Published and distributed in the United States of America by:
Hay House, Inc., PO Box 5100, Carlsbad, CA 92018-5100. Tel.: (1) 760 431 7695 or
(800) 654 5126; Fax: (1) 760 431 6948 or (800) 650 5115. www.hayhouse.com

Published and distributed in Australia by:
Hay House Australia Ltd, 18/36 Ralph St, Alexandria NSW 2015. Tel.: (61) 2 9669 4299;
Fax: (61) 2 9669 4144. www.hayhouse.com.au

Published and distributed in the Republic of South Africa by:
Hay House SA (Pty), Ltd, PO Box 990, Witkoppen 2068. Tel./Fax: (27) 11 467 8904.
www.hayhouse.co.za

Published and distributed in India by:
Hay House Publishers India, Muskaan Complex, Plot No.3, B-2, Vasant Kunj, New Delhi
– 110 070. Tel.: (91) 11 4176 1620; Fax: (91) 11 4176 1630. www.hayhouse.co.in

Distributed in Canada by:
Raincoast, 9050 Shaughnessy St, Vancouver, BC V6P 6E5. Tel.: (1) 604 323 7100;
Fax: (1) 604 323 2600

© Jenny Smedley, 2010

A catalogue record for this book is available from the British Library.

ISBN 978-1-84850-162-1

Printed and bound in the UK by CPI Bookmarque, Croydon, CR0 4TD.

All of the papers used in this product are recyclable, and made from wood grown in managed,
sustainable forests and manufactured at mills certified to ISO 14001 and/or EMAS.

As always, I thank my husband Tony for his forbearance and undeniable help as a proofreader. I also thank Barbara Vesey for the hard work she put into editing this book. I thank my angels for their ongoing help and patience.

Contents

Preface

Have you ever jokingly said, 'I must have been someone really good (or bad!) to have the life I'm living now?' Deep inside, do you seriously wonder if you might have had one or more past lives? Or perhaps you do believe in past lives, and often wonder who you might have been and whether it makes any difference to how you live today.

I can answer some of your questions right away: Yes, you *have* had past lives, and yes, they *do* affect your current life. How do I know this without even knowing your name? I know you have had past lives because, for you to be aware enough even to ask the question, you must also have had past lives, or you wouldn't be so spiritually open. As for past lives affecting your current life, I can answer yes, they do, because they always do affect every one of us in one way or another.

Just as your childhood in this life helped mould you into the person you are now, mentally and emotionally, so past lives moulded your soul into the emotional and energetic way it is now. Just as a childhood trauma in this life can leave you damaged in some way, or lead you down to emerge into this life damaged in some way. Of course it can work in reverse, too: Some special talent or gift developed over the course of a previous life can mean that you started this one with a big head-start, being incredibly and unnaturally talented, as with a child prodigy.

A belief in reincarnation (having had one or many past lives and having returned to another physical body after each death) is the single most common creed in the world, and roughly 75 per cent of the world's population accept it as a fact. Whether you are one of those 75 per cent who believe in reincarnation or not, you will have at least heard of the concept of karma and balance. The wonderfully funny TV show, *My Name Is Earl,* depicts someone who believes his life will be good if he completes the tasks on a list that contains all the bad deeds he's done in his life and what he needs to do to make up for them. He believes that karma governs every move he makes, and that if he makes the right move he'll be rewarded, and if he makes the wrong move he'll be punished. The show doesn't have it all right, of course, but this comical look at karma has at least brought the concept into mainstream television.

Karma isn't really about crime and punishment or good deeds and reward; it's more like a balance sheet of wisdom, and that wisdom is what we learn through our multiple lives and the various lessons we experience in them.

The more these lessons from the past are accepted and understood, the greater our capacity to have a trouble-free and even blessed current life. If you're curious about your past lives and the state of your karma, and if the concept that perhaps your past lives could hold the key to current life happiness interests you, then this book will help you understand important truths that may be missing from your existence.

Do you believe in angels? Perhaps you'd like to, but you need a firm concept that you can come to grips with rather than the common thinking that angels are unreachable beings that don't really have anything to do with you. Did you ever think that there might be some special angel you could really relate to and that might help guide you through lifetimes? Did you ever think that you could have a relationship with an angel that was as close as ... well, having a relationship with yourself? Well, you can, and these beings are what this book is really about. I call them *Soul Angels*.

Introduction

My first encounter with what I now call my Soul Angel – although at the time I had no idea that that's what it was – was back in 1993. I'd been slowly going downhill as regards emotional strength, or lack of it, for quite a few years by then. I'd felt for some time that something was missing from my life, and I'd been casting around, trying various hobbies and projects, in an attempt to fill the void I felt growing inside me. Nothing fed me. Nothing made me feel fulfilled or contented. I felt that there must be something 'out there' that would satisfy my mysterious and unnameable need, when all the time the answer wasn't 'out there' at all, it was *inside* me. The answer lay deep in my soul, but I hadn't learned to access that part of me yet. My soul's need had gradually spread throughout my entire being, making me depressed and unhappy, filling me with darkness, but I wasn't able, and didn't know how, to see the cause of it. My Soul Angel knew, and tried to open the doors of communication. I'm sure it must have started at that time with dreams, but they obviously weren't strong enough to break through my barriers. So the next step taken by my Soul Angel was to send me a recurrent nightmare. This nightmare was real and extremely terrifying. I'd never had one before that I was so 'present' in. This is how the nightmare unfolded, and in it I thought in a turn of phrase that was entirely different to the way I speak now. That was just one of the mysteries of this nocturnal experience:

I'm walking through dense woodland with a thick and impenetrable canopy of branches overhead. It's a sunny day, but the trees make an effective parasol and it's as dark as twilight, reducing visibility to a few dozen yards. I can feel the hem of a long dress dragging through the grass, and this is a surprise because I never wear dresses, long or short, and yet it feels familiar. Its weight, hanging from my waist, feels familiar, as does the feel of the stiff lace that's pricking the soft skin of my neck. Every detail is real. I can smell the greenery around me and touch the odd leaf as I push through. I can feel my hair on my head, pulled tight, and if I put my hand to it, instead of the loose long strands I normally feel, there are round, glossy-feeling beads and fine net, over hair that's bound up in some way.

I'm going to meet someone, and I know he won't be too pleased with me for wandering this far from the house alone. But he'll be pleased to see me at the same time. The woods seem peaceful and secret as I walk with pleasure. I'm looking forward to meeting 'him'.

But suddenly the atmosphere is changed, and a prickle of fear tickles my spine, because I hear a noise behind me. I stop walking and listen, and there's a quick rustle behind me. I look back but I can't see anyone in the shifting shadows. I walk on. Then I hear the noise again and I know that some creature is following me. It must be a human – no deer would stalk a human. Now the quiet woods seem filled with menace and I feel very alone and vulnerable.

My heart starts to hammer and I grow cold. I start to hurry, thinking that I'll soon be in earshot of Ryan, and then I'll be safe from whoever follows me. I hear the noises again, coming closer, and now whoever it is has thrown caution to the wind. I don't know what to do, whether to shout, to run, or to turn and fight.

Suddenly it's all too late. Hands grab me from behind and I fall over, landing heavily on my back, knocking the wind out of me. A heavy weight crashes on top on me, making it impossible to draw breath or scream. Then, there he is, in my face, the man who's been hunting me down. He's revolting. He grimaces, showing blackened and yellowing teeth. His forehead is etched with purple veins that stand out. His hair is smelly and dirty and his skin pockmarked under a scruffy beard. He's panting with lust, his face above mine red and fevered with it. His breath is so foul that I have to turn away as the stench fills my mouth. He shifts his grips to my hair and my right hand, to stop my futile attempts to lash out. I still try to hit him with my free left hand, but my muscles have no strength and my fist flutters uselessly.

One of his hands leaves my hair and delves downwards. In horror I feel it pulling up my skirt, and then his scratchy nails scrape up my inner thigh. I want to die, right now.

Then I hear a voice cry out in the distance, 'Madeleine!'

The very sound of the voice revitalizes me. It's Ryan! Strength fills me and I clench my left hand into talons, drawing blood from my attacker's face. He hesitates. Now, finally, I can breathe, and I yell as loudly as I can, 'Ryan! Ryan! Help me!'

At that point in the nightmare I always woke up, hot and sweaty and scared. My lovely husband, Tony, always comforted me, and by morning, although I could still conjure the fear I'd felt when I thought of the events of the nightmare, I was a bit calmer – and very puzzled. Who was Ryan? Was I the Madeleine he called out to? How could that be? Why was I wearing clothes I'd never worn before, clothes that didn't fit with the age I currently lived in? I dreaded that nightmare, which came at regular intervals. It never quite left me, and whenever I thought about it too much, the terror I'd experienced during it rose up into my throat, making me feel ill, because it was so real that I thought it might be a premonition – something that was going to happen to me in the near future. Little did I know at the time that the nightmare was actually created by my Soul Angel, who had been working very hard and forcefully, using a deep-seated past-life memory to try and capture my attention. After a while, I suppose when that didn't seem to be achieving anything much except scaring me half to death, another nightmare reared its head.

In this one I was walking through a very old house, filled with dark, huge furniture of another age. I felt incredibly sad, desperate and alone. I'd walk up the stairs following something or someone, who remained just out of sight or appeared misty, like a ghost. Eventually I'd emerge into the attic room and then I'd cross to the window, open it, climb out onto the roof, and stare down. Only then would I see who it was that I'd been following: A ghostly shape of a man materialized. A spirit or a ghost, I wasn't sure which, stood below on the ground, his arms open wide. With no fear, crying out that same name, 'Ryan', I'd jump off the roof. As I met the ground I'd realize that there was no one there to catch me, and white light would suddenly burst in my head, waking me up. The main mystery, as from the previous nightmare, was who was Ryan? I'd never known anyone by that name. Why would the sight of him below induce me to jump into mid-air and certain death?

It was that second nightmare I think that put the word 'suicide' into my head as a distinct possibility, a way out of my depression. I wondered if perhaps the nightmares were created by my subconscious trying to show me an escape route from the growing shadows in my mind. Of course that wasn't the intention of my Soul Angel at all, and when I found myself sitting alone one afternoon contemplating such a thing and only being held back by the love of my husband and son, my angel took another route to get me to listen.

I think that depression can sometimes open the mind to possibilities that would otherwise be rejected, and so it was with me. I was suddenly filled with a quivering thought, that something amazing was about to happen. The hopeful inkling was a straw to clutch onto. I'd often prayed to God for help, and now I suddenly felt He was going to answer me. He was going to tell me something that would change everything. I waited, breathless with anticipation. The words formed, in my mind or out loud, I've never been quite sure, and the words – these words that would change the whole universe for me – were, 'Turn the television on.' Oh. What a letdown. Not the words I was expecting to hear from God at all! Nevertheless, undaunted, I obeyed them.

The TV flickered into life and a man's face appeared on the screen. I didn't know him, and yet, I *did*, inside out and front to back, with no doubt and under every imaginable circumstance. That fact I was immediately 100 per cent sure of. Smiling blue eyes reached deep into my soul, and though I didn't understand it at the time, turned back the pages on my own history to a time when those eyes, and their owner, had meant more than life to me. All I knew that day, though, was that the shadows in my mind fled in that second of recognition. I had no idea at the time how or why that could be. It just was. Tony, and Phillip, our son, were both amazed at the instant and dramatic change in me. I soon discovered that the mystery man on the TV was an American singer called Garth Brooks, but why he should have had such a dramatic effect on me remained a mystery. It wasn't a fan thing. I didn't collect his photos or long for an autograph. Yes his songs had meaning for me – some of the lyrics spoke volumes – but that wasn't it. The reason for my depression lifting was just the *recognition* of the man himself.

For months I was happy just with the change in me, but eventually I was driven (as I found out later) by my Soul Angel, to seek more answers. I needed to know why the man's appearance in my home via the medium of TV had banished my depression. I needed to know why I suddenly started to shed, effortlessly, my excess three stones in weight. I needed to know why a floodgate of creativity had been opened in me, to the extent that within months I had penned a song, which had been recorded, released and won a silver disc. I needed to know why I'd been transported back to the happiness of childhood when miracles were expected and accepted as normal. I needed to know, and yet I was afraid. I was afraid of what I might discover. I somehow knew that my journey to recovery and happiness wasn't over, but just beginning, and I knew that something dark was to be endured before I could emerge fully back into the light.

It took one of those people, those 'teachers' who come into our lives momentarily, obviously angel-sent, to point out what should have been a very obvious signpost to us, who said that perhaps I'd known this man in a past life. She suggested that perhaps Garth had been the elusive Ryan, and that I'd recognized him in his new, and yet very similar, physical body. The eyes, as they say, truly can be the windows to the soul, especially when it comes to past-life recognition. Needing to understand, I finally did what my Soul Angel had been trying to get me to do for years. I investigated and invested in myself. I went for regression therapy under hypnosis, and discovered the truth of my past, and found that I was right to sense that revelations would contain some dark moments.

I found that I'd been Madeleine, a young English woman of French Catholic descent. I'd lived in the 17th century in Hambledon in Hampshire, in a house Tony and I subsequently found. Ryan had been a young Irishman, on the run from his blue-blooded, jealous half-brother. After falling helplessly in love, against the wishes of my parents, Ryan and I (as Madeleine), ran away and got married and, for my part, though not his, remained completely unaware of the depth of my parents' disapproval, and the evil lengths they were willing to go to, to cancel the marriage. They eventually had Ryan abducted, sent to fight a war that was none of his doing, and then betrayed him to his half-brother, who followed him into battle and killed him.

During Madeleine and Ryan's time together, the attempted rape, committed by a knife-sharpener from the village festival, and the one that I'd dreamed of, took place. It was followed later, after Ryan's disappearance, by Madeleine's suicide. She jumped from the roof, in her near madness, thinking it was into the safety of Ryan's arms.

It took some while to get my head around all this. To accept that I'd lived before and that I'd known a man who in this life had reincarnated into a new body, as I had. At this point I had no idea that there was an 'external' force guiding my path towards total knowledge of myself.

As you can imagine, while my emotions floated about happily on the one hand, knowing that fear of death was a thing of the past, on the other hand I wanted to go and meet this 'Ryan', now known as Garth. Knowing he was reborn was great, but my grief at losing him as Ryan, which had patently lasted hundreds of years, was too deep-seated to be totally cured by seeing his flickering image on a TV screen. As anyone who had a loved one restored back to life would be, I was eager to see him in the flesh, to grasp his hand and heal the wound that had been created hundreds of years previously, when Ryan and Madeleine's hands had been torn apart.

It wasn't that easy, because although here in the UK most people hadn't heard of Garth Brooks, in the USA he was probably the most famous star after Michael Jackson. I got a bit impatient with all that, all the walls that surrounded him, all the pomp and barriers that 'celebrity status' created. To me he was just 'Ryan', a poor, powerless yet charismatic young Irishman, torn from his home, rootless, and someone I had known intimately and loved desperately. I knew I didn't love him the same way today, in his new body, and there would be no physical chemistry between us, because he and I were not meant to be together in this life, and I had my soul mate in Tony. Still, it seemed a bit annoying that in this life he was pretty much unreachable and certainly, it appeared, untouchable. His management, while not exactly hostile, weren't about to give me any help. I'm sure they were afraid I'd sully their golden goose with what they felt were 'flaky' notions of previous existences. Perhaps I was after 300-odd years of alimony – yes, that was the way their minds worked, so it was little wonder they wanted to keep me at arm's length. But by now I knew that it didn't really matter what they wanted; what was meant to happen would happen, and I was sure this was meant – this circle closing, possibly for both of us.

Garth Brooks appeared, on the media-driven surface, to be happily married, but I was to discover that all was not as it seemed, and that he too needed freeing from the past.

So, I overcame a life-long phobia of flying, took no notice of the fact that Garth's management were against us meeting, ignored the information I had been given that he wasn't at his home near Nashville but was in Los Angeles, went to Goodlettsville, found his house (with a little angelic intervention) and got to do what I knew had to be done – to grasp his hand in mine and close the circle. He was as open-minded as I knew he'd be, showering me with gifts and finding the whole concept of having had a past life totally fascinating.

Following this joining of hands, things went on to change for me dramatically, but also for him, too. He finally accepted that his marriage had faded, found the courage to admit to the world and his fans that he wanted a divorce, and quite soon afterwards, married his 'this life' soul mate. I believe he hadn't been able to take that step before because his past as Ryan had made him incapable of walking away from what he saw as his responsibilities. In that past life he'd left his wife, Madeleine, despite his vow never to leave while he lived. It hadn't been his fault, and no one could ever have blamed him for being abducted against his will, but it had still left him with a feeling that above all else he had to be trustworthy and he had to be reliable, and he had to never give up on his marriage. But I believe that the rejoining of our hands freed him to see that it was in everyone's best interests this time around that he did leave his wife. And so it proved to be. He ended up with his true love. Happy endings all round. One thing I'd contracted to do in this life had been ticked off my list, just like with Earl's list in the TV show.

It wasn't long after this that I was visited by a Master Path angel. This angel appeared to me in a vision and showed me my major role in life, my reason for being born again into this world. I was to be a spiritual seed-planter. I was able to receive this information at last because I had taken steps, such as overcoming my fear and flying to the USA, and so I was ready to take up my major role.

* * * * *

It took me some while to understand what I was being told I was to do, along with all the past-life information. What was a seed-planter, and how did one become one?

What it was turned out to be simple. It merely meant trying to plant a seed of spirituality within people's hearts. It didn't have to be any particular brand of spirituality, such as a belief in reincarnation, just a seed that would make them start to re-evaluate their lives and their priorities. To perhaps have them regain hope in something more than just the winning post of the rat race.

I have been nudged and guided along the way of how to be a seed-planter, right up until this present day. I first found myself some friends – a lot of them members of my soul group (souls we interact with over many, and sometimes all, of our lifetimes), as it turned out – by seeking alternative believers in my local town. And I started off simply, doing card readings for people. This in turn led to my occasionally, and then more often and more easily, being able to 'see' other people's past lives. I always believed, and I still do, that no one should foist a reading on another person without a request to do so, but it sometimes made me giggle when people would walk into the New Age shop I worked in at the time, and their clothes would just shift and change into old-fashioned outfits from their past lives right in front of my eyes. It was quite hard to understand why they themselves didn't seem to notice anything! Of course, if they asked, I told them. One particular time I recall telling a woman I could see her in a crinoline gown and dancing slippers, with her hair all up in ringlets, only for her to tell me that this was exactly what she'd already seen under past-life regression. Of course, for a while I thought perhaps I was getting the information from the people's own minds, but then there'd be cases when they'd only get corroborating information *after* they'd been to see me, later on down the line when they'd finally been regressed.

At this time I also discovered a little about how we can reshape reality, and that there was something very powerful underlying our physical persona, although at that time I had no idea how dramatic that 'something' would actually turn out to be. It began when I spoke to a friend who'd been striving for a few years to breed a 'coloured' foal. That is, a horse patterned fairly evenly in black and white or brown and white. She'd used all sorts of colour combinations of mares and stallions to try and achieve this, but to no avail. Finally, the year before, she'd acquired a chestnut mare that had already produced a beautiful coloured foal by a certain black-and-white stallion. So she'd put the mare back to the same stallion and confidently sat back to wait. When the colt was born he was chestnut, just like his mother. She put the mare back in foal again and just hoped it would be second time lucky.

During this time we spoke about what I was coming to believe – that we could shape our own lives – but she was a total cynic. She told me, 'If we can change reality, then you make the next foal coloured for me!' It was a challenge I had no idea if I could meet, but I decided to try. I did a sketch of the foal. I saw it first as a whole chestnut, then I visualized pouring hair-colouring bleach over it to take out some of the brown. The bleach ran round the neck, forming a white collar. I dripped some on the face and made a narrow white stripe there. Next I created a white patch on one side of the neck, and on the belly on the opposite side. I knew my friend wanted the foal to have four white stockings, but I could only get at three legs with my bleach, as one hind leg was mostly tucked underneath the foal where he lay in his mother's belly, with just the foot and pastern showing, so I drew three white stockings and one white sock on the legs. I drew in all the markings I'd 'created', and finished it off with a distinct white lightning flash on the rump. Several months later my friend called me in high excitement to say that she finally had her coloured foal. I rushed round with my drawing and we compared it with the real foal. To everyone's amazement – mine included! – the markings matched up. It was extraordinary.

Another incredible event gave me yet another clue to the power we all have hidden inside us. I 'saw' in a meditation a brown-and-white springer spaniel dog. The dog ran past me where I was standing next to our car, his lead trailing, and next minute there was a sickening bang and he was lying in the gutter, having been hit by a car. I love dogs and it was an awful vision to have. I recognized the place as being the car park and main road of our nearest village, Loddon, and I told Tony all about the dream. A few days later we were in the car park there, having just got out of our parked car, right next to the section of road I'd seen in my vision. Something made me turn, just in time to see someone climbing down from a red 4 x 4. As they did so, a brown-and-white springer spaniel jumped from the car and ran towards us, and straight at the road. Because of the forewarning of my vision, I was ready for him, and as he whipped past I grabbed his dangling lead. I held on fast and pulled him to a stop a yard or two from the kerb and the whizzing cars. The owners were very grateful, although of course they weren't to know that their dog would have ended up dead if not for my vision. Tony and I were astounded, though.

However, at that time I still hadn't tied together my past life, Soul Angels, or where this ability to sometimes change reality came from. At that time I was just enjoying the magical ride.

Since my Master Path angel had shown me my role as spiritual seed-planter, I'd accepted it and taken my first baby steps along my rightful path. As usually happens with people, I was then given some skills to help me accomplish my role. One such skill was being able to create aura photos from ordinary pictures, and the other was to create angel portraits in a digital medium. It all started off quietly, like my past-life readings. I created some abstract digital paintings, just for fun, and people started to say, 'There's an angel in this one, look.' Gradually, as I embraced this gift, the angels got clearer and clearer. Finally, they were honest-to-goodness, actual pictures of angels. I started to create unique portraits of people's angels and used them to give more detailed past-life readings, because I'd come to realize that the angels related closely to a person's past life.

After a while I thought I'd completely understood the concept of the angel who had brought me messages, at the time calling them 'past-life angels' rather than Soul Angels. I'd said (and I was right) that these were a legion of angels whose duty was to be next to a particular soul, from the time it was just a spark in the clay, right through every lifetime and in between lives, guiding and nudging that soul along and helping it decide on the appropriate next life to achieve the most and best progress. In all of that I was right, but apparently I just didn't go far enough. What I did already know, and accept now, is that angels like to surprise us, and recently I got a very big surprise, and it's the reason behind this new book. I was drawn to meditate, quite forcefully. What often happens in these instances is that I'm made to feel quite weak and tired, to the point where I simply have to go and lie down. As soon as I do I'm transported, and sometimes, as with this recent incident, I receive an insight of such stunning new knowledge that I am left gasping in amazement, and full of angelically inspired joy. This latest insight was what compelled me to give the 'past-life' angels their entirely more appropriate name of Soul Angels, and begin helping *them* to help *you* find true happiness.

CHAPTER 1

What Are Angels?

OUR USUAL PERCEPTION OF ANGELS

Before I begin telling you in detail about Soul Angels specifically, and their purpose in being in our lives, I need to write a bit in general about angels to set the scene.

It's said that angels are divine beings who can communicate directly with God, and are messengers sent on His behalf. What does this actually mean? To me it means that angels are beings made up purely of light and energy. They generally exist in a higher dimension than we do. This dimension is one we can never enter – not while we remain physical and human, because our natural vibration is not capable of being upgraded to a level high enough for us to survive in their realm in a physical form.

Angels can manipulate their energy to appear in whatever form they deem appropriate; if they choose they can enter our dimension and visit us, or sometimes we can change our vibration enough to allow our energy to separate from our body enough to enter a dimension that exists halfway between their natural habitat and ours, in which they can meet us.

God exists in a higher dimension yet – one that even angels can enter only with effort. But what is God? To me God is a power, supernatural (to us), and the guiding and powerful force that controls the universe. I don't believe He naturally exists as an old man with a beard as in biblical portrayals, but can appear in any form He wishes to. I particularly like His portrayal in the book, *The Shack*, in which He is a jolly, wise black woman. His natural form is probably nothing that we can possibly imagine.

This is where it gets difficult, because, as you can see, I've found it necessary to refer to God as 'He'. This of course is a total misnomer, because God most certainly does *not* have a gender. However, it would seem impolite and impersonal to call God 'it', even though that is probably more correct, so for the sake of comfort I'll continue to refer to God as 'He'.

God is also known as the 'observer', and in this aspect we on Earth play a role that is greater than we might imagine. We become God's 'observers' here, through the use of our 'third eyes'. These 'virtual eyes' are our psychic centres, and they are sited in the middle of our foreheads. Even if you're not aware of having this psychic ability, you still use it on a subconscious level to send 'reports' or observations back to God because He can make use of you with or without your knowledge or conscious co-operation through His connection to you: your soul. The soul is your connector to God, to spirit, and the only part of you that can never die.

To try and prove that you can be God's observer I have to delve briefly into what physicists call 'the measurement problem'. Put very simply, this means that in experiments in the quantum field (molecular level), the results differ depending on whether an experiment is 'observed' or not. In other words, the molecules appear to behave differently according to whether or not there is an 'observer' present, which could be any one of us, in person or even through the use of a camera. The theory is that God uses us to observe every aspect of this universe – we are His eyes, no matter whether we believe in God, psychic ability, or the power of angels and the universe.

This also then proves that we do indeed have the power to change reality. The greatest atheist in the world is still God's observer, whether he knows it or believes it or not.

This leads me also to say that as far as I am personally concerned, God actually *is* the universe. By this I mean that 'God' is within every molecule and cell. This of course means that I also believe that every molecule and cell is part of the intelligent whole that forms the Universe and … God. This unity is important to my belief in Soul Angels and what they are. The revelation I had regarding them slotted everything very neatly into place, and once I'd got over the initial awe-inspiring truth, I realized that in fact it had always been quite obvious. You only have to look at evolution. It's one thing to say that every living thing on this planet evolved from the same DNA, but when you look at the diversity of life, and the way that animals and humans have been so cleverly 'designed' (I use that word deliberately), it becomes obvious that either we have been manipulated by an outside force, or the very molecules and cells we are all made of decided to implement changes themselves.

Take, for example, the bat. It had to evolve, in a very short space of time, into an animal that could not only fly accurately directed by its own inbuilt sonar, but also catch its prey using the same system. At the same time, its prey had to evolve to keep step with it. I am reliably informed by scientific colleagues that this is as likely to have happened randomly as it would be for a tornado to hit a junkyard and accidentally assemble a fully working space shuttle. So, our cells, and therefore ourselves, are part of the intelligent, divine whole, which confirms the existence of Soul Angels, as I'll reveal later.

So, back to the general view of angels, who are accepted in all forms of religion, in various guises. From Christianity to Islam and from Judaism to Zoroastrianism, angels have survived all worldly upheavals and, today, there are more people who believe in them than not. In 2002 there was a study investigating whether or not people in the UK believed in angelic beings, and a catalogue was done of those who said they have had experience of an angel. There were various sightings, sometimes with multiple witnesses present, of angels who appeared to give a warning of some danger that could be avoided, actual physical interventions where a person was pushed or lifted out of the path of danger, or given messages of hope and unexpected joy in the midst of a sorrowful situation. These angels, when they appeared, wore various disguises, from classic winged beings of light to old ladies and young men, even children at times.

A survey in the USA in 2008 carried out by Baylor University's Institute for Studies of Religion discovered that 55 per cent of Americans believe that they have been protected by a guardian angel during their life. These accounts feature even those people who claim to have no specific religious beliefs.

I've had several encounters with angels now, and each time they've appeared differently to me than they did the time before. I've also become aware that there are many different realms of angels, and their appearance is often governed by the nature of the particular group they're a member of.

Archangels, or Master Path angels as I prefer to call them, in my experience usually appear as a column of glorious light, usually white or golden. They have no discernable form and they are often more felt than seen. They normally appear at moments of life-changing proportion, and occasionally will be heard speaking, even if they don't actually make an appearance.

Guardian angels more often have appeared to me in traditional 'winged being' form, usually as a rather beautiful young man.

On one occasion in particular I didn't see the angel at all, but I felt its influence. It happened at my dad's deathbed. This experience underlined my beliefs so beautifully, and made me able to accept Dad's passing with manageable grief, unlike when my mum had died several years previously, which had left me totally devastated for the next four years. I sometimes wonder whether if I'd been with my mum when she died, I might have seen the same thing as I did with Dad. On the other hand, I wasn't spiritually awake then, so maybe I wouldn't have been able to see it even if I had been present.

At the time of my dad's passing, Tony and I lived on the other side of the country from the nursing home where Dad lived near to other members of the family, and times were hard for us then. I knew that I could only afford to make the trip once, so I wanted to make sure it was at the right time. It was a six-hour train ride to Norfolk. Dad was suffering from a very miserable condition called motor neurone disease, and it was so far advanced that we knew he didn't have very long. I wanted to try and make sure I was with him when he died, and so I was waiting for a sign that the time had come for me to make the trip. Some family members berated me for not going to see Dad on several occasions, but I knew that he'd want me to be there to see him off, so I carried on waiting for a sign.

Finally, one day an angel whispered in my ear that it was time to go, and that my dad was just waiting to see me before he let go of his life. I set off immediately that day, and when I reached the nursing home I was pretty shocked that my dad, who, when I'd seen him a month or so earlier was still mobile and talking, was by then helpless in bed, unable to move or speak, and deeply under the merciful pain-controlling influence of morphine. I sat and talked to him, making sure he knew I was there, thinking back to, and already grieving for, the vibrant, sport-obsessed man he used to be. He didn't respond, wasn't able to respond, apart from a grunt just to let me know he knew I was there. I thought of how as a child I'd watched him play cricket, a love of his life, and how we'd all marvelled at his stamina and ability, which was retained even into his seventies, to beat youngsters at his second favourite sport, badminton.

To see a man previously so strong, and on whom I'd relied for that strength through most of my life, in such a weak and helpless state was terrible, and I was glad for him that he'd soon be out of the body that had become so useless to him. I was heartbroken that I was losing my dad, but I didn't want him to suffer any more. I knew he'd be better off in spirit, with Mum. After a couple of hours I went to my son's house, where I was staying overnight, to get some sleep, but I had barely made it there when my sister rang to say that I needed to go back to the home right away.

The nurse told us that Dad was fading, and we settled in to wait. At about 5 am, I was sitting in the chair across from the bed, not comfortable enough to sleep but letting myself drift into a hypnogogic state to get some emotional support from my guides and angels. I felt that they were going to help me, to give me something that would make me able to cope with my impending loss, but I was little expecting the miracle they were about to show me. I felt angelic love surrounding me, accompanied by the tingling expectancy I always feel as some form of communication is imminent, and then it happened.

I clearly saw myself rise up from my chair and walk to the bed where Dad lay. I was transparent, because what I was seeing was my astral body rather than my physical one, which stayed sitting in the chair. I approached the bed and Dad's spirit sat up, which his physical form was incapable of doing. I reached him, sat down with him, and we hugged. It felt wonderful. He felt strong, his arms just as powerful as they'd been throughout my childhood. After a few moments, my astral body walked back to the chair and sank back into my body.

I looked back at my dad and I saw that his spirit had risen to a standing position. He was still attached by his feet, and although his spirit struggled, it could not break free from its physical shell.

I felt so happy, though, because I knew without any doubt that Dad not only wanted to go, but that he *had somewhere* to go to, somewhere he couldn't wait to be. I felt so relaxed that I was able to go to another room to sleep on a sofa. Two hours later I was awoken and told it was time. I hurried back to my dad, and after a few minutes he breathed his last. I saw a flash of light out of the corner of my eye that whipped up and out through the glass of the closed window, and knew that Dad had escaped at last and had gone to the light.

At the moment of death my dad's body immediately assumed a wax-like appearance as his spirit left him. There was no point in crying, although of course I did; he wasn't there any more. He was in a better place.

This experience affected me so much that for the first time at a funeral, I was able to detach from the normal horror of imagining your loved one inside the coffin. I could remember how devastated I'd been when my mum's coffin had been there in front of me, and then later at the cemetery how I'd been unable to believe that it was really her they were lowering into the ground.

Dad's funeral was a special occasion because of all the people who came to say goodbye, and it was sad because I had to accept that I would never see my dad, as my dad, ever again. However, the coffin itself meant little to me, nor did the remains inside. I knew that, like a caterpillar turning into a butterfly, Dad had metamorphosed into something *much* more wonderful than the discarded shell he'd left behind. Dad wasn't in that box; he was above us, around us, chuckling with his wicked sense of humour at what his friends were saying about him.

When the coffin was placed into the ground, I had to curb my impatience at the lack of purpose to it all. We were burying a wooden box with an empty shell inside it. I was actually excited for Dad, trying to imagine where he was now, and also knowing that there would always be a part of him watching over me. Even if he was reincarnated at some point, a part of him would remain in spirit, a guardian over me. How could I be grief-stricken at that thought?

This is just one example of what angels can do for us in times of need, if we listen and if we hear them. Those who close their eyes and ears will also close their hearts, and deprive themselves of miracles.

ARCHANGELS/MASTER PATH ANGELS

Traditionally there are 15 named Archangels, or Master Path angels. These are the angels who can show you what you came here to do, but this only usually happens if, like me, you've responded to your Soul Angels.

Michael: Known as the leader of angels, the first one created by God. He is said to help all Earth-bound lightworkers (those who teach and encourage spirituality) and also to be a powerful defender who can be called upon in times of fear and despair.

Raphael: Known as the healing angel, to be prayed to in times of illness and disease. He is also called upon to help with arduous journeys, whether of the spirit or of actual travels of the body.

Gabriel: This is the only Archangel shown in pictures to be female. While of course angels are actually genderless, the feminine form alludes to this angel's skills with helping parents, especially those trying unsuccessfully to conceive a child. Gabriel is also said to be the angel best for helping with spiritual issues.

Uriel: The creative angel, very useful at filling your mind with solutions to problems, or new business innovations. Uriel is also known to bring warning, helping people avoid great disasters.

Chamuel: This is the angel people pray to for help with relationship problems. This can be relationships of a romantic nature, or between friends and family members. If you need to find the right words to heal a rift, then this is said to be the angel you need.

Jophiel: The angel of artists and musicians, Jophiel is said to be very helpful when it comes to feeding your creative juices. He will also bring you insight when it comes to teaching others.

Raguel: This angel is said to dispense judgement and justice should the other angels not be able to agree on a fair course of action. Raguel is also the angel to pray to if you feel that no one else will listen and that you're being treated unfairly, either at work or in the home.

Ariel: This angel often appears in the form of a lion or a magical, mystical creature, such as a fairy. At one with nature, Ariel can be called upon to help injured wild animals.

Azrael: This is the angel I believe showed me my dad's peaceful and joyful release after death. This is also the angel many claim to have seen at the site of great tragedies, such as the 9/11 bombing, carrying the souls of the dying upwards.

Camael: Like Michael, this angel is said to have the ear of God. This angel is said to be able to help prevent war and should be prayed to at times of global conflict.

Haniel: This angel can be called on especially when trying to use crystals and natural remedies to heal. He is also useful when you need extra confidence, such as when you have to deliver a speech or do some kind of public speaking.

Jeremiel: This angel brings us visions, and is the one called upon by mediums and psychics to help them work within God's grace. He will also help show you your whole life and the good and bad you've performed in it, after you have passed into spirit.

Metatron: This, it is said, is the angel God uses when deciding which souls should die at any particular time. Metatron can bring messages warning of death, should this be deemed necessary by the Creator.

Raziel: The overseer of the workings of the universe. It is he who has brought knowledge to the world of the existence of the quantum universe and all that it implies.

Sandalphon: Many believe that this angel is the one who conveys their prayers to God. He is also said to escort souls up into Heaven.

Having listed all these names, I have to say that I think names are actually totally irrelevant for angels. I've often said that, in many ways, animals are more spiritually evolved than humans. One way I can demonstrate this is that animals don't give each other names. We're the only species on earth that does this. Both angels and animals are foreigners to the concept of having to give a name to those they love. However unique you think the name you choose for your child is, somewhere in the world there will be someone else with the same name, and sometimes hundreds and thousands of them, so it's rather foolish in many ways to allow or need a name to define us. Angels and animals recognize others by their energy, not by their label. We seem to need this distinction, whereas they do not. If we were able to 'see' energy all the time, and transmit it freely to each other, as we once were, then we wouldn't need a name for anyone. We'd just be able to 'think' the energy of the person or pet we were visualizing and the other person (or the pet) would know exactly who we meant. Not only that, but we would have a much clearer picture of who that person really was.

So, while there's no harm in giving angels names, and it can be useful to our mindset to distinguish them in this way, it only goes to pinpoint our lack of real understanding of the state of spirit, and just how much we've become detached from our true being.

GUARDIAN ANGELS

It is thought that every soul on the planet has a specially assigned angel to protect them personally, and this being is called their guardian angel. Each person, when they are born, has an angel allocated to them, and can call upon it through prayer and meditation. It's also said, though, that even your guardian angel can only help you if *you* ask for help. You can't ask for help from someone else's guardian angel on their behalf, as their angel is not allowed to change that person's path without that person's permission and a request from them to do so.

'ODD JOB' ANGELS

Just as they sound, these beings are around on Earth all the time and can help you with little 'odd jobs', such as finding lost items, mending broken devices or finding you a parking space in a crowded car park.

CHAPTER 2

What Are Soul Angels?

'All the world's a stage, and all the men and women merely players ...'

WILLIAM SHAKESPEARE

WHAT IS THE SOUL?

The soul is that unseen part of us that connects us to the universe, to God. The soul is that little flame of spirit that burns within us all and is always joined to the realm of angels by a tenuous thread. The soul is that part of us which leaves our dying body, as has been seen by some as a translucent form striving to leave the corporeal body. If you've ever been with someone as their soul has left, as I was with my dad, you'll have seen their physical envelope suddenly transformed as if into a waxwork, and you'll have known, as I did, that the element that made your loved one your unique loved one, was no longer in the body. Some scientists have even claimed that the human body loses weight immediately at the point of death. It's just a couple of ounces, but it's been enough to make them wonder if it's indicative of the soul leaving the body and if it means that the soul can actually be measured in weight. The soul is the immortal part of us, the part that returns to the Creator after our bodies have expired. The soul is the part of us that is poured into another body at the right time, so that we can live again as a human. It is the part of us all that progresses, and eventually becomes so balanced that it no longer needs to return to a physical body.

When Shakespeare wrote the words quoted above, he was closer to a spiritual truth than he perhaps knew. To explain what Soul Angels are, I have to first set the scene of your life, and also to assemble the cast.

THE STAGE AND THE STAR

The stage is this world, and your life is the current play that's showing. Before this life you have been the 'star' in many other plays, many other lives. There's a good chance you will go on to star in many other plays before you leave this world for the last time and reside in spirit, a balanced and completed soul. Your current life will become less worrying and stressful for you if you remember this. Before you were born you 'wrote' the script for your lifetime. While 'down here' in a human body, it all seems very vital and quite frightening at times, but from your place in spirit it would appear trivial, because you'd understand that it's only a fraction of you that is suffering the slings and arrows of being human. This life is just a learning experience for you, set up by you, as were all the others.

THE DIRECTOR

This is also you. To be a successful director, you'll have to step out of the cast, put aside emotional weakness and control rather than endure. You can imagine, if we are indeed the director of our own life play, then of course we are capable of changing the script – but we rarely do so. It takes effort and faith, and we're often sadly short of the faith to have the commitment to put in the effort. (More about this later.)

THE SUPPORTING CAST
SOUL MATES

There are many theories as to what soul mates are. To me, because of my experiences, I believe you can have several soul mates, and several different kinds of soul mates. Some will be partners from previous lives, who just come into your current life momentarily to fulfil a contract they made with you, before you were both born, to help you in some way. And, if you're meant to have a close partner in this life, one of your soul mates will be that person. Having more than one soul mate, and more than one kind of soul mate, can make things very confusing, as this account from Moira from Vancouver demonstrates.

'I'd been struggling with my relationship with my husband for years, wanting to make the marriage a success, feeling it was right, and yet feeling a lack of any kind of passionate connection between me and my husband. I resented his calm and even temperament for some reason. He made me feel sometimes like a naughty child and I was starting to feel that I wanted out of the marriage, even though I loved him. I wanted to try regression to see if there was a reason for my feelings and, hopefully, be able to put them behind me.'

I'm Tommy, a 12-year-old boy, and I live with my mother. We don't have much of the material things. However we share plenty of joy, laughter and love. My mother does everything to provide a loving and supportive environment for me. I couldn't ask for a better mom.

We're best friends and do everything together, from exploring the outdoors to cleaning the house. We totally love and adore each other.

'I recognized my present husband in Tommy's mother. At the end of the session my therapist asked me to feel Tommy's mother's love, and to bring that unconditional love into my present life.

'After the session I felt very confused. I'd expected and almost hoped to find something bad and nasty, but instead I was given a feeling of overwhelming love and peace. I've never left the marriage, because from that time I started to see my husband in a different light. Whatever I had perceived as coldness became an acceptance and space. The lack of excitement turned into a quiet tenderness. Three years later, we had a baby girl.'

I feel that the block between these two was caused by Moira's subconscious knowing that her husband had once been her mother. This brought conflicted feelings through and made the connection seem wrong somehow, which in turn eventually led to Moira looking into her past lives. This is an example of the complications that can arise, but with a skilled therapist's help the feelings can be understood and turned around.

SOUL GROUPS OR SOUL CLANS

When we're first an energy spark in the clay, we're laid alongside all the other members of our *soul clan*. This makes great sense, because these are the souls that are going to match our own progress and re-enact with us, life after life, and so we start next to them and journey along, side by side, progressing up the life chain, sometimes closely linked and sometimes further apart, but always connected.

These are groups of souls which by now you'll probably have encountered over and over again in past lives. You'll often recognize them when you meet them in a life, but probably won't know why. Members of this soul group might have been asked by you to play a sweet and supporting role. Perhaps they'll have a position of great power, for instance, and have agreed to give you a 'leg up' on your path. Or they might have agreed to play an aggressive or otherwise 'dark' role in your life, if you've decided you need certain negative events to happen to you. They will do this out of love, on a soul level, even though they won't like to.

SPIRIT GUIDES

These are spirits you once knew as humans, who have agreed to remain in spirit to help and guide you through difficult times. These guides are often members of your soul group who have passed to spirit while you've remained on earth. They can also be deceased relatives who feel that they want to continue to help you. They can do this because they have been beyond and returned with memories fully intact, and they know the truth.

SOUL ANGELS

Every one of us is born with a 'soul manual' – a sort of set of instructions that we need to follow in life to help our soul progress and walk our rightful path. We learn it by heart just before we are born. We have discussed with our past-life angel what parents we need to be born to, the time of our birth, what we are meant to achieve as regards soul progress in this life, and then we are thrust into our human bodies. But this is where the trouble starts.

When we are born, we still remember what we've been taught and what our carefully thought-out plans were. But as we grow, we are changed. Our parents, peers, teachers, friends and society in general all change us. They all mean well, they all want to help us fit into society, but what it means is that we start to forget our roots. We want to fit in, so we stifle anything unique or different about ourselves for fear that we won't be accepted. We see it all the time: teenagers, believing they're rebelling and being true to themselves, actually mimic their peers and all end up wearing what amounts to a uniform, no matter how outrageous it might at first appear. We all become 'fashion victims'. We become social victims, too, feeling we need all the same things everyone else has to make our mark in the world. We busily strive to earn money and prestige and amass possessions that will 'prove' our worth to ourselves and to others.

Everyone falls into the same trap. They're born and then they grow up being wrenched away from their soul. They are taught to concentrate on winning the rat race, or to feel incomplete unless they have all the trappings of conventional success, which are totally material in nature. And, if you look back, that's exactly what our ancestors did thousands of years ago – and where are all their belongings now? They are being dug up out of curiosity by archaeologists. Apart from that, they mean very little, and nothing at all to the people who strove to collect them. This earthly classroom never really changes.

We totally lose sight of what we really came here to do and what really matters, and our past-life angels are left frustrated, just as they always have been, life after life, as their charges fall off the right path and follow the route of 'normality'. At this point we become 'normal' humans, divided from our true selves. We see the world through the human filter of need and greed and material possessions, or hardship and loneliness, and we often feel unloved because we are no longer able to see that there is someone who has always loved us – we let go of our soul, and in doing so we let go of our connection to God, to the universe, to that unseen presence that has always loved and will always love us, no matter what. In this state we are virtually blinded by the worst of all human emotions – fear – and we just can't see the truth. We live in a world of infinite beauty, where a field of wheat can be transformed into a sea of molten gold by rain, and where the sky can become a moving film of heavenly swirling colours. This world is populated with animals so diverse that they simply cannot have arrived here by accident. We share our lives with incredible creatures such as dogs, whose connection to their Creator is constant, and yet our fear rarely allows us to appreciate any of it, because we're divided from the part of us that is connected, not only to God but to everything in the universe. If we could see how immense we really are, we wouldn't waste a second worrying, and we'd treasure every moment of wonder that's available to us. The angels spend all their time trying to jog us back on track, shock us into recall. They do this through a variety of means, not all of which are nice. No fluffy angels, these. No pretty white wings or golden halos. These angels are nothing if not ruthless. But no wonder, because the reward their charges gain if they're successful is worth so much. To restore that lost connection, so that we see the universe and ourselves as they all really are, is priceless. To reunite us with our souls is a much greater prize than anything imaginable. The angels also act as if their very future depends on it, and one of the things I've learned recently is that it really does, and much more so than I could ever have imagined.

These angels might send us dreams or spontaneous visions of our past lives, for they know that the best way to 'wake us up' is for us to recall the whole of our history, not just what we remember from this life. They need us to shake off the amnesia of the soul (which we all develop) and remember what we came here for. Just as someone with amnesia in this lifetime wouldn't be able to function properly without understanding their own history, our souls cannot function properly without understanding our distant history – all the pages back to the time we lay in the clay as a mere spark.

If the gentle nudges don't work, then these angels will up the ante, bringing us nightmare memories, illnesses that correspond to our past-life traumas, scars on our body to remind us of our past-life wounds. They will even cause us to repeat destructive patterns of behaviour, because to them reuniting us with our souls is more important than any discomfort, either emotional or physical, in this brief foray into the human world that is our life.

You might ask why this happens. Why don't we remember everything? Surely that would be possible? Yes, it would be possible, but there are some practical reasons why it wouldn't be acceptable. When babies are born, imagine if they had total recall. Imagine how frightening it would be to remember all the people you'd been and all the lives you'd lived, and yet be lying helpless in a cot or buggy, completely at the whim of the people who are your parents. Certainly, such a child would have enormous difficulty growing up, or regarding its parents as anything other than temporary caretakers. No genuine bonds could be formed.

It's true that some children do have some recall as they pass through years two to seven, but it's rarely anything concrete, and by age seven all memories start to fade. You might ask why they have to fade. Why don't we retain childhood glimpses of past lives into adulthood? There are practical difficulties there, too. Imagine remembering all the people you've ever known before. You might, for instance, remember your sister as having once been your husband, or your friend having once been your mother. You wouldn't be able to interact properly with them or form the new relationships with them that you were meant to. You'd also recall all the languages you'd ever spoken, which could be mentally impossible to handle.

Then of course there's the real reason, the most important reason why our memories are stripped from us: If they weren't, then we wouldn't face our greatest challenge, the one we came here to conquer. This is the challenge of reuniting with our soul, and it's a challenge we can only experience in the envelope of a human body. For, unlike any other creature on Earth, humans live their lives fragmented by the human condition. Mind, body and soul are disunited. Intuition is stifled. The challenge is to reunite these facets of ourselves, and to do it amid all the machinations and abominations that exist in the world of mortal men, both inside, in the realm of the emotions, and outside in the world. Once we face our challenge and overcome it, bringing forth our whole being in a united and balanced front, then we make our angels very happy. This will lead to us remembering and understanding our true purpose in this life, and that will make *us* very happy.

There are two kinds of happiness. One relies on influences outside ourselves, and is subject to disruption by other people and events outside our control. The other kind, the enduring kind, is generated from within and cannot be disrupted by outside influences. This second kind is inviolable, and it is the kind we would all cherish above all else. This second kind of happiness comes from fulfilment, that feeling we get when we start to achieve our life's purpose.

If we don't discover the second kind of happiness and how to get it – what happens then? We'll spend life in the pursuit, not of true happiness, but of stuff that we *think* will make us happy. Stuff that we can't take with us, like money, houses, cars, clothes, while all the time we ignore the right stuff – the stuff that we *can* take with us: spiritual wealth, a balanced soul and abundant, real happiness.

The most important thing that we really forget when we come here, the thing that changes everything when we do remember, is this: We are never fully on the earth plane. Our whole self is never really human, or even mortal. That which exists here, in the physical, is only a tiny, tiny fraction of what we really are. The main part of us, the important part of us, never leaves the spirit world. This fact is what started me waking up to what I'd missed in my theory of past-life angels.

As I've said, I thought I'd understood fully the concept of past-life angels, until I was shown the real truth. The reason I changed how I refer to them, from past-life angels to Soul Angels, is that I was shown, in my recent meditation, that these angels are *us*. What others have called our higher self is actually our divine self. That divine part of us is more magical and more wonderful than people have dreamed. That part of us is actually angelic. These angels are not ethereal messengers from God, unreachable and untouchable by us mere mortals. These angels are not in another league from us. These angels are not incomprehensible beings of pure energy which we can only gaze at adoringly. *Each and every one of us is a facet of an angel.* We're only 'mere mortals' while we're on this world; our roots are not only spiritual, they are angelic.

Once I got over the shock of this revelation, I was shown how it all came about.

Many, many thousands of years ago, it was decided by the universe, or God, or whatever you feel happiest calling the supreme power, that further evolution had to take place in the universe. To this end it was decided that the angels needed a catalyst to push them into a new design. So, some fledgling angels were created that could detach a part of themselves, which could then become a soul. This soul could reside in a physical body, on a planet, whereas the angels themselves are of course pure energy. This was done in the same way that all matter was created: by turning some of the energy into light.

If you doubt this possibility, take another look at the Big Bang theory, the creation, according to scientists, of the universe. I always wanted to ask a scientist: If this theory is true – if the entire universe came from an explosion of matter – then what was there before? One internet source gives the definition of the Big Bang as: *A cosmological theory holding that the universe originated approximately 20 billion years ago from the violent explosion of a very small agglomeration of matter of extremely high density and temperature.* The key words for me are 'very small'. How is it possible that the entire universe came from a very small blob of matter? If it did, what was there before? Because it seems that we got something from nothing, or very nearly. The answer seems to me, although I'm not a scientist, to be that the origins of the Big Bang were created within the *energy* trapped in the dense matter. This energy was changed into light (just like a light bulb converts electrical energy into light).

In the same way, part of these fledgling angels' energy had to be changed into light matter to create a soul. This soul, at first just a tiny spark, would then be placed in a physical receptacle in order that it might experience and grow in a way that angelic pure energy cannot. At first the empty soul would be divided up into many primitive life-forms, such as plants or insects. Once it had been 'coloured' and slightly 'filled out' by its experiences, then it would return to the host, decide (with the help of its Soul Angel) on the next appropriate life, which would move it higher up the 'food chain', and then return once more to the physical. This would happen over and over again, with the soul continually returning to and evolving the angel it originated from. Gradually the soul would be divided into a smaller and smaller number of fragments until it reached the top of the 'food chain'. At that point human reincarnation would start for the soul, and its further education and the angel's further evolution would continue for up to 85 human lives. This is the universe's plan for angels to evolve, and we poor weak humans are, amazingly, a major part of the process. The new angels are the energy, and we are the light. Together we form a whole greater than the sum of our two parts.

This knowledge stunned me, and made me gasp in amazement as no other angelic teaching has ever done before. To think that we are actually created by angel dust, and will return eventually to be reabsorbed into our angel hosts, is mind-boggling.

It changes everything, and it also explains a lot. It's been known for years that even when we're alive on the planet in a physical body whether it be as an animal or human, a part of us still remains in spirit. My experience of this came when I received messages through mediums from various passed-over spirits, even though I knew they'd been reincarnated and were once again living on Earth.

For instance, I had messages from Ryan, even though his human essence was alive again in the body of Garth Brooks. The messages were indisputably from him, even though the medium, Steven Holbrook, had no knowledge of the details of my past life with Ryan.

I already knew that this spiritual presence was in fact the *main* part of us, but I didn't realize that it was also angelic in nature. This new understanding brought a great change in me, for I came to see that if we are part of an angel then we are indeed the masters and makers of our own destiny. We are much more powerful that we ever knew.

This understanding made me able to answer the questions I get asked, such as, 'I have a terrible life. Why would I choose that?' Of course, once we're in spirit and reunited with our angelic part, the part of us that endures life on this Earth has one single purpose, that of evolution. This explains why we would opt for bad things to happen to us, because this life is far more of a classroom than I'd realized. Our angelic self is not concerned with making life easy or pleasant; it's totally focused on how our souls can evolve in their physical envelope and bring about the evolution of angels at the same time. So, this is why it's up to us to change our reality for the better, by calling in our own angelic power rather than relying on angels outside us to make life nicer for us.

This also explains why sometimes dear ones who have passed over don't seem to hear our pleas for a message to assure us that they're OK, or that when they do it can seem to take a long time before we hear anything. When you consider that after each death our soul reverts to its pure angel form for a while, until all it has learned has been assimilated by that divine self, it's not really surprising that what's going on back on the Earth plane fades in importance and significance. It's not that our departed loved ones don't care about us any more. In fact, it's quite the reverse. It's because we too have our divine part in spirit, which they have instant access to after they've died, and so to them we have never been parted, and there is no need to speak to us in our physical, earth-bound form.

I found this all very comforting, because it means that babies, for instance, who die are never alone or without the protection of their parents. In fact they are instantly reunited with the divine part of their parents as soon as they cross over, and so are never parted from them. We don't have to worry about being greeted by loved ones when we die. We will be greeted by them, be they living or dead, but we will also be greeted by our own divinity.

It also made sense to me of the fact that there are people on this planet who, if you really look at them, show the angel puppet-master behind the strings. The Dalai Lama is probably as close to an angelic presence that it's possible to become while still remaining in a human body. His Soul Angel shines through for all to see, and so I believe he must be on, or nearing, his 85th lifetime. One day we will 'become'. Our divine selves will outshine even the archangels, and this is what makes our journey through many lives, with all their trials and tribulations, worthwhile.

Of course, this also answers some of the greatest questions of all time:

WHY ARE WE HERE?

We are here to take part in the evolution of angels by allowing our souls, which are a part of them, to experience that which can only be experienced in a physical body. We are here to take steps in the journey towards divinity, and each lifetime is one step. It's up to us to make sure that step takes us in the right direction.

WHY IS THE EARTH HERE?

The Earth was created by turning energy into light to provide us with a stage to live out our dramas on, and a school of learning. There may be other planets where the same thing is happening.

WHO CREATED IT AND US?

The entire universe has intelligence within every molecule, and they are capable of making a collective decision to take these steps. This is confirmed by the fact that although science has proven that on a quantum (microscopic) level all matter is fluid, it chooses to retain its apparently solid form in order to make a functioning world. This collective intelligence can be manifested as a single, thinking entity – hence the belief in a God who cannot be seen.

WHAT HAPPENS WHEN OUR SOUL IS BALANCED?

If we return over and over to balance our souls, then what happens when they don't need to return here any more? Our souls return to their source, which by then will be an evolved form of angel.

Having said all of that, now I realize how powerful the 'director' of our play is, being part of a divine being. I can also see why spiritual gurus tell us that we can change the script of our lives to make things easier for ourselves, once we have accomplished the lessons we came here to learn. We can do this simply by acknowledging the lessons and, as director, rewriting the script.

This is where our past lives come into the picture, because by understanding what went before, we can grasp what lessons we have come here again to learn.

And also, past-life recall will help us to discover our Master Plan by enabling us to reunite mind, body and spirit, thus becoming closer to our angelic base. From there, every tiny step taken on the path to that plan will bring us happiness that comes from deep within us, through knowing we're fulfilling that plan.

One other thing I'd like to comment on is that, judging by the portraits I'm guided to produce of these angels, they comprise almost always, predominantly, female energy. This is because female energy is the energy of Home. In this instance, 'home' is the Primal Source, the power behind the universe.

CHAPTER 3

Past Lives and Soul Angels

Since I've become aware of them, I've always sensed that Soul Angels depend on our progress for their own. It makes more sense now that I know how much this really is true. Our progress is the governing factor in their evolution. It's not surprising, then, that your Soul Angel will use all means to jolt you into remembrance, because with remembrance comes progress. In order for your Soul Angel to evolve in the way the universe intended, it must succeed at its task. That task is to bring your soul into balance so that you and it can be reunited.

Balance is achieved only when we become fully reconnected to our soul, and the best way for that to happen is to persuade us to access our *Akashic records*. The word *Akashic* is Sanskrit and refers to the etheric substratum of the universe. It's said that a permanent record of every single event, sound, sight or thought that has occurred during the entire history of creation is stamped upon this electro-spiritual substance. Therefore these records will contain all our past-life experiences and so can bring us back to full memory. Also, once these memories are accepted and known, they can also lead us beyond, to where we are aware of our whole being so that we can recall our life's purpose.

Our life's purpose doesn't need to be of world-shaking importance. It's not a question of discovering that you're meant to be a famous person, or perform amazing feats, although of course it can be. It's a question of feeling satisfied, deeply contented through fulfilment, which creates happiness from within. For instance, some people feel they should be doing something more than they are. They feel dissatisfied with their achievements, which makes them anxious and unhappy. It can be that there is some path they're meant to tread, some amazing things they're meant to do, and until they make a start on whatever it is they can't be truly happy. Or it may be that they're not meant to do anything more than be a great parent, perhaps to make up for being a less than perfect one in a past life, or to create a wonderful garden, both of which they were already doing but didn't feel was enough of an achievement. Once they know they are fulfilling their contract, the one they agreed to before they were born, suddenly what they had perceived as a 'minor role' will fill them with contentment and they'll stop miserably trying to achieve more than they need to, and understand that their role *is* important.

Soul Angels have one major way to communicate with you and help you. They operate just as people have described the 'higher self' as operating: they hold access to all of your Akashic records, the database of all your past lives. Because they have all this information they're able to target you with nudges that will work. Traumatic or very happy incidents are etched firmly in your subconscious. Very strong emotionally responsive events will 'float' quite near the top of your memory files, and so they are easiest to trigger and be used as a nudge. For instance, if you had a very painful death that was caused by a devastating injury, you might develop a pain at that site, triggered by your Soul Angel accessing that floating memory. Or you might have experienced a very joyous event in a past life, centred for instance around the birth of a longed-for child. In this life your nudge might then consist of an obsession to give birth, despite perhaps enormous fertility problems, and this trigger will take over your life. It might cause you to sacrifice everything else in your life, your home for instance, to make what you see as your dream come true.

In actuality your subconscious may just be driving you to recreate that feeling of joy you had in a past life, and your Soul Angel may be using this device as a way of reminding you of your past.

Here's an example of a classic past-life nudge, when a past-life trauma causes a chronic pain that can't be cured by 'normal' medicine. It comes from Dr Georgina Cannon. This example gives convincing evidence that these traumas are utilized by our Soul Angels and manifested by them into symptoms to nudge us onto our right path.

'Ever since my early teens I'd regularly suffered from severe migraine attacks. The pain usually started on the left side of my head, just behind my eye, and then it spread all around to the back of my head. I'd always assumed that these migraines were the result of physical battering I'd had from my mother – who I now know was emotionally unstable. But that's a whole other story! These migraines were debilitating in the extreme. The warning signal always came from my stomach, a churning sense of fear that moved up my body within seconds, and then exploded into extreme pain, dizziness and nausea. Sometimes I was out of commission for two or three days – not helpful for school studies or my work track record.

'As I got older and moved away from home and started exploring a different world, I decided to find alternative ways to deal with the migraines. I went for vitamin therapy and for a while the headaches subsided, but never completely went away. I tried aromatherapy, colour therapy, meditation, pure will-power and pain medications. Each "solution" worked partially for a while, and then the headaches would become unbearably severe again. I saw many doctors, specialists and healers. Nothing seemed to work.

'I grew up in England, and for me, believing in the supernatural is a given. I believe there are fairies at the bottom of the garden, and ghosts at Hampton Court Palace. I understand that we can talk to or communicate with "the other side". And I also know that, real or not, as long as there's a healing or closure, that's all that really matters.

'In 1997 I chose to give up the corporate world and become a hypnotherapist – a practitioner and teacher, opening a clinic and a school. It was a no-brainer to move on to working with past life regression, the "interlife" and spirit and entity-release work.

'One day in class, a past-life regression led me into the life of a woman in what looked and felt like medieval England. I could see a small village nestled in a circle between hills. The village was surrounded by farmers' fields and seemed to be very primitive. Although I could see the village, I didn't feel part of it, and on further exploration discovered that I lived by myself in a cave on the side of a hill, as a witch or crone.

'It was hard to tell my age. Close to starving, I depended on the villagers for food. I was so dirty I could smell myself! My hair was filthy and matted. Very much an outcast, I was lonely and lived in fear. The women of the village would leave me bits of food from time to time so that I'd live and help them with their birthings and illnesses.

'My role, my job, was to help women give birth, and also to give abortions. I spent my time collecting herbs and making potions to encourage easy births, or painless abortions. From time to time men would visit me secretly at night, and ask for some herbal cure for their impotence. But always I was treated with disdain and made to feel less than the animals in the fields.

'One day I was called into the village to help a woman give birth. It was a difficult one, and nothing I did would stop the bleeding. The child – a baby girl – was healthy, but the woman died in childbirth. Not an unusual experience in those days. That night, under cover of darkness, her husband came into my cave. He was obviously drunk. He was yelling and throwing stones at me. I moved to the back of the cave, crouched down in fear, trying to protect myself. He picked up a large rock and smashed at the left side of my skull with that rock until I died.

'As my soul left that body, I was encouraged to forgive the man, remembering he behaved the only way he knew how ... and leave the pain of that life behind.

'Since that journey, I have never had another migraine.'

It really can be that dramatic. Give your Soul Angel what it wants – accept the lesson or recall the reason for being the way you've been – and the problem can vanish in an instant.

Here is another example of past-life trauma causing a physical symptom, which was used by a Soul Angel to good effect. The release of this trauma by past-life regression also removed a blockage in the person's function in this life. It also went on to show how two members of the same soul group will come back together in order to help and support one another in some way.

Andrea, from Sheffield, was a healer at her local spiritualist church, but she had a problem that was stopping her being as effective as she could have been. Whenever she was healing someone, or being healed by someone else, she'd develop a pain in her lower stomach area. It could be so severe that she'd have to stop the healing. She went to a past-life therapist for regression, and this was what she discovered.

> *I'm a man, a soldier in the American Civil War. The scene around me is dreadful. The blood, the extreme noise and chaos as guns fire, and all I can smell is death. I'm severely wounded and in terrible pain. I'm lying in a hospital tent, as all around doctors try to tend to the dying and the wounded. They too are covered in blood, and they run around, panic-stricken themselves. Men are screaming. I was hit by a cannon shot and the ball passed right through my abdomen. I know I can't survive.*

At that point Andrea was in such pain that the therapist asked her soul to leave her body. They then both asked for the karmic cords to be cut and that Andrea be released from any negativity that may have been attaching itself to her in this life.

Andrea had come for her regression with a friend, Bethany, and at this point it was Bethany's turn for regression. The two friends did not talk between the sessions, so at this point Bethany had no idea what Andrea had seen.

> *It's the time of the American Civil War and I'm hiding behind a rock watching a battle. I watch in horror and feel*

unable to move, even to look around. I'm a young Native American girl, and I see all of my family being killed in front of my eyes. My father put me in this hiding place and told me not to move and not to speak to anyone, before he went out to die.

A few weeks later the therapist received a card from Andrea, telling her that since the regression her pain had gone completely, leaving her free to heal and be healed. She was so impressed by what had happened, knowing by then that Bethany had watched the same battle she had been killed in, that she'd decided, in her mid-sixties, that she was going to train to do hypnotherapy and take up past-life regression.

I was told of another miraculous incident from Lesley in Cardiff:

'I'd always suffered from asthma, ever since I was a small child. I daren't go anywhere without my inhaler. Over the years many "cures" have been tried, the most effective being giving up cow's milk and changing to goat's milk. But still I suffered attacks. I was particularly susceptible to car fumes and any trip to a big city was fraught with fear and danger. I'd pack three inhalers just in case. It wasn't until I was 25 that someone suggested I investigate the possibility that a past life might have some bearing on the issue. I was happy to try anything, really, because I felt very disabled by my condition and it stopped me doing many things. I'd always wanted to start mountain climbing, but I just didn't dare risk getting stuck halfway up somewhere, having an asthma attack. During regression, this was what happened.'

I can't breathe. My chest is on fire, a crushing sensation is all I'm aware of. ('The regressionist took me back a few minutes.')

I'm driving along in a car. I'm feeling quite happy, humming to the radio and driving perhaps a little too fast. I'm driving alongside a big dyke in Cambridge, where I live. Suddenly there's a bang and the steering wheel starts to spin in my hands. I can't keep the car straight, and braking doesn't have much effect. As I think about it I realize that I have a puncture – maybe two. The car sails up into the air and everything becomes very quiet and like slow motion.

Then there's a huge splash and my teeth clash together, almost biting my tongue off. The car is still rolling and ends up upside-down in the water. It sinks. I'm trapped by the crushed dashboard and I can't get out. The water fills my mouth and swirls coldly into my stomach. It fills my pipes and lungs and I can't breathe. It grows darker and darker, and then there's a blinding light.

When Lesley came round she realized that her asthma symptoms were very similar to how she'd felt in the car as she was drowning and being crushed. She'd felt she couldn't draw air into her lungs. Because she'd already resolved her dairy intolerance, her asthma disappeared overnight, and within a year she was climbing quite challenging peaks.

PAST LIVES AND CRUELTY

This knowledge that we ourselves, in our angelic form, are responsible for the events that overtake us in our current lives makes sense of the apparent cruelty of some of the things that existence, both past and present, throws at us. These events lose their cruelty in the light of my discovery, and come to make sense. It becomes obvious they are actually sent by *us,* for *our* higher good. It's very hard for us trapped down here in our mortal bodies to see the whole picture, but of course our divine selves, our Soul Angels, can see it all very clearly. They see the end-game and pretty much focus on that above all else.

PAST LIVES AND PUNISHMENT

I have so many people writing to me asking if they did something bad in a past life that they are being punished for in this one. Again, my new understanding proves the lie to that. We are the only ones who judge us, and even then we do not judge our own actions, but rather we judge the *effects* of the past life and current life on our souls, and clearly see the next direction that needs to be taken to redress any imbalance, and the experiences we need to go through in order to accomplish this. In this way we ourselves design our next life to suit those criteria, and those criteria alone.

PAST LIVES AND GUILT

Whom should we forgive? What is the most important place to start for karmic purity? People would probably suggest those who have wronged us in past lives, but this is not necessary. Anger towards those we have shared past lives with is naturally filtered out during the time we spend in between lives. Our Soul Angels take us through this process so that we can move on.

The place to start forgiving is with ourselves. Guilt is the most destructive of all emotions. It leaves us crippled with doubt and fears, and often makes us incapable of enjoying relationships with past-life soul group members or anyone at all.

This guilt makes us feel undeserving of love or happiness, and can cause all nature of self-destructive behaviour patterns. We can sabotage ourselves, and the most common manifestation of this is when we constantly destroy approaching happiness. One way this often happens is by the person becoming a severe hypochondriac, constantly imagining deathly illnesses at the first sign of a joyful event. Or they might become a compulsive obsessive, not realizing that the rituals they feel obliged to employ to keep everyone and everything safe are just ways to assuage their underlying guilt. We do this subconsciously, maybe, but deliberately nevertheless.

Even someone who was a mass murderer in a past life, even someone like Adolf Hitler, for instance, should not bring through guilt to their next lifetime. It is totally counterproductive. That past existence is over and a line should be drawn under it. The only thing that should be considered from that life are the *effects* it had on the person's soul and what needs to happen in the next life to ensure that soul progresses along the right path. Because of this, people should never be worried about having past-life regression because they might uncover something unpalatable about a past life. The therapy is not about that, and it should comfort anyone to know that all of us who are, in this life, balanced and spiritual will have led lives of all natures in the past. Living a wide variety of lives is the only way to become a balanced soul.

Guilt is misplaced, because anything we've done, any crime we've committed in a past life, is not our responsibility now. We are not that soul – we merely *evolved* from that soul. Taking the blame for its actions would be like a bird taking the blame for something a dinosaur did. These things we did in past lives were designed to bring the greatest benefit to our souls, and there can be no blame for that.

So, we do need to learn from our mistakes and experiences, but to carry the blame for them through the next life is unnecessary and blocks our progress in the worst possible way.

My own example of this was that I blamed myself for the murder of my husband in a life in the 1600s. I thought that it was dangerous to love me, because in that life, had he not loved me, then he would not have died. In this life it resulted in my not being able to enjoy the first several years of my marriage because I was constantly afraid Tony would be taken from me, and always terribly jealous and insecure because I thought I did not deserve to be loved. I constantly doubted that love, and another partner might have left me because of the intensity of this doubt.

Luckily for me, once I was regressed to fully understand my part in past events, and my naivety in that life, I was able to see where my guilt came from, and understand how I was sabotaging myself because of it. I was able to see that I could forgive, and that though I was indeed partly to blame for the incident, it was attached to a part of me that no longer existed. I had evolved, and so forgiveness was possible. This enabled me to stop the self-destructive behaviour immediately.

Sometimes we suffer from guilt and sometimes other people treat us as if we're guilty. In this instance below, Brian, from Vancouver, was being made to suffer for something he did when his soul was in another body.

Brian had nine siblings. Family bonds were strong and important to him. He got along with everyone in his big family except his younger brother, Peter. For some inexplicable reason Peter couldn't stand Brian, and didn't want to do anything with him for as long as Brian could remember. At every family gathering they ended up with a big confrontation. For the last ten years they'd been avoiding each other and finally stopped any attempt at communication. But this standoff had to be broken because the family was planning a big celebration for the 60th wedding anniversary of their parents, and the whole family was coming. Brian decided to go for past-life regression to see if it would uncover a possible explanation of this feud with his brother.

My name is Raymond and it's the early 1930s in France.
I have a best friend, Jean-Paul. ('I recognize Jean-Paul

as being my brother, Peter, from my current lifetime.')
Jean-Paul and I were inseparable and we vowed to be
friends for ever and stay always loyal to each other. Life
became increasingly difficult, confused and dangerous
as the war years approached and people were hunted
down. I found myself making a choice. To save myself
I lied and betrayed Jean-Paul. Jean-Paul was prosecuted
and sentenced to death. I lived the rest of that life trying
to justify my actions.

It's obvious that the betrayal in that previous lifetime
never was resolved, and came through as a residue into
their current life, where they are now brothers. By carrying
through the guilt he had from a past life, Brian was actually the one putting up barriers between himself and his
brother, even though he didn't realize he was doing it. He
didn't think he deserved his brother's love.

At the end of the session Brian's therapist did some
powerful forgiveness work with him, until the whole
healing of the Second World War life was completed.
Brian realized that the lesson of the Second World War
life was to experience making a bad judgement and the
consequences of that decision, and having the courage to
admit it. Brian contacted his therapist several weeks after
the big family celebration. At the gathering Peter and Brian

had made a connection and engaged in harmonious small talk. They decided to keep in touch. Brian has recently received an email from his brother.

CHAPTER 4

Your Own History Lesson

HOW DO YOU KNOW IF YOUR SOUL ANGEL IS 'NUDGING' YOU?

Past-life recall not only holds the key to reuniting mind, body and soul, but also to healing past-life traumas that are affecting current lives. These sufferings and more pleasant nudges are sent to us by our Soul Angel in order to jolt us into a different mindset, so that we'll be receptive to taking steps to recover our soul balance. But sometimes these nudges can be distressing and uncomfortable at the very least, and show themselves as trauma for which there is no discernable cause. They are therefore incurable by any 'normal' means.

The ways to know if you're suffering from these are myriad, uncountable. Almost every problem encountered in life for which there is no explicable reason can be attributed to past-life traumas. During my work as past-life reader 'Dear Madeleine' in *Chat – It's Fate* magazine, I'm often called upon to give people karmic readings to explain how they are being affected by past-life traumas. Here are just some examples of the questions I've answered either psychically or by using my past-life therapist training and regressing the subject under hypnosis. Some accounts have been provided by other therapists from all around the world.

PHOBIAS

Phobias are one of the most common devices used by Soul Angels to give us nudges, so this section has a lot of examples. People can quite often suffer terror at the mere sight of something apparently innocuous. I'm not talking about fear of spiders or snakes, which could be race memories, or a fear of something that's harmless in itself and yet considered fairly natural, such as darkness. I'm talking about something that seems really silly to other people, such as a fear of balloons or a fear of leaves. These things make no sense to friends, who are inclined to laugh and even sometimes use the fear to play tricks on the victim to amuse themselves. They really can't understand how someone could have such a silly fear, and so they can be quite cruel. These phobias will have been sent to the person from their Soul Angel, in other words from *themselves.* Just the fact of seeing this for what it really is can greatly reduce the terror, for how can a person really be that scared of something they gave themselves? There can't be any real harm in it for you, can there? Then the next step would be to follow the lead of their Soul Angel and take themselves back to when and where that fear was originally created. By doing so, probably through past-life regression, they'll be fulfilling their Soul Angel's needs by reconnecting their mind, body and spirit, and thereby will take away the need for the fear as a nudge to wake them up to their real self. This step can eliminate the phobia entirely, and even if it doesn't, remembering what gave them the fear will give them knowledge, and this will create the power they need to squash the 'inexplicable' fear for good.

Sally from Dorset had a fear of leaves that couldn't be explained. Nothing in her childhood had ever happened to give her what seemed like a totally irrational fear. Leaves are not dangerous in any way, and yet she felt a deep, incapacitating fear of them. It was always worse in the autumn. The colours and beauty of autumn leaves were wasted on her because she couldn't bear to look at them. Sally had had all kinds of treatments, both medical and psychological, but none had really worked. She couldn't understand why just the dry rustle of autumn leaves could induce a state of physical collapse in her, so great was her fear. When she was a child, the other children, as they do, quickly sensed her fear and capitalized on it in the ever-challenging arena of establishing pecking order that runs through most playgrounds. They'd throw leaves at her and laugh as she scurried off screaming. They didn't understand her fear and so they couldn't sympathize with it. Finally, Sally wrote to me and I was able to help her. This is the story she recalled under hypnosis.

> *I'm in a forest. It's warm, the air's warm on my skin. I'm very scared, listening for something. I know that men are chasing me, but I don't know why. My mind is closed down in dread and won't let me understand. All I know is that I cannot be found. As I stumble on, this fear of being hunted, of being nothing more to them than a prey animal, makes me shake and my blood screams at me to run, just run! But I'm on foot. I can see my feet and they're bare. I can feel the twigs underfoot and the occasional nettle stinging and pricking the skin. My feet are bleeding, but I can't stop. Those hunting me are on horseback, and my terror increases as I hear the dreaded sound of baying – they have dogs! They'll follow the scent of the blood from my feet! I'm a woman. I can feel my body as*

I run on. It's hopeless, though. They will catch me. I'm going to die, horribly, and they'll use me both before and probably after I'm dead. I can hardly breathe and I wish I could find a cliff that I might throw myself off to escape the inevitable, but there's nowhere to hide.

Eventually, I cannot run any further. I'm going to die, and I don't even know why. I see a gulley ahead, filled with last autumn's leaves. They look deep and I plunge into them, praying that I might find a miraculous hiding place in there. I can hear the thudding of my heart over the sound of the leaves crunching under my bare feet. I am up to my thighs now in leaves, so I drop to the ground and start to burrow into them like an animal. The leaves close over my head and I snuggle down into them, pulling them over me. I feel that no one will see me, and if the dogs don't find my scent, then maybe there's a chance.

Minutes pass and I hear nothing. I start to hope, and the tiny seed grows in my heart as the minutes tick by and still I hear nothing. My breathing has slowed and my heart rate has fallen below that of a hunted deer. Then it happens, I can hear a slight crackling sound and I know they have found me. The sound grows louder as if they're stomping through the crispy leaves. My heart starts to flounder again as I can almost feel their hands upon me. No one touches me, though, but the sound grows louder and louder. Suddenly excruciating pain clutches at my feet and legs and I'm forced to jump to my feet. I'm surrounded by flames that greedily eat the dead leaves! They have set fire to the leaves with me inside! They surround me in a circle, laughing as I try and get away from the burning pain.

Now an arrow pierces my stomach and many hands reach for me, pulling me from the leaves to whatever awaits me in their clutches. Half-dead already, the last thing I hear before I lose consciousness is the sound of the brittle leaves as they blacken in the flames, and the sound as my body is dragged through the leaves by rough hands … I'm so afraid.

When Soul Angels use a phobia to nudge us, it's always generated by something that we once experienced. In Sally's case it's easy to see why the sound of leaves was something she feared, even in this life. Her terror at the moment of capture, and the pain from the burning, were symbolized by the sound of crispy leaves. Once she understood the reason for her fear, it melted away like hot butter, because she knew that her current life was nothing like the life she'd recalled, and that now, leaves should hold no terror for her.

Lisa from Telford had been afraid of dogs all her life. She was interested in having past-life regression to see if that might pinpoint the cause and help her quash her fear. However, she kept the specifics of her phobia to herself beforehand.

My name is Jacob and I'm 11 years old. The year is 1309 and I live in Edinburgh in Scotland. Right now it's just a little mud village.

Later I marry a beautiful girl named Emma. There is only one downside to this. For some reason we don't know, her father hates me and never gives us peace. I work for a while as groundskeeper to his estate/house. In the end we have to leave as his cruelty gets too much to bear. I don't think he ever forgave me for taking his little girl away.

My death in this life is horrific. Emma's dad sets his huntsmen and wolfhounds on me and they pursue me through the woods. I die when they bring me down and rip me to shreds, with Emma held back, screaming.

'I was so shocked at this when I came out of the hypnosis. I hadn't said a word to the regressionist about my fear of dogs. One only has to come near me and I start to panic and hyperventilate. I've lost count how many times a dog has bitten me because they've sensed my fear. Sadly I've unwillingly passed this fear on to my little boy.

He tries to climb me like I'm a tree if a dog crosses his path. I understand now that this fear has come from that past life, and I am able to be calmer around dogs.'

Sometimes someone suffers from a classic phobia. What I mean by this is that there are phobias that have a 99 per cent chance of coming from a similar scenario. One such is a phobia of vomiting and of seeing someone vomit. I don't mean the often normal reaction of perhaps feeling sick yourself when you see someone be sick, but a reaction of utter and abject terror. The sort of reaction you might perhaps have if you were receiving a hopeless prognosis from a doctor, or facing a man with a gun pointing at your head. One such person was Gill from Purfleet.

It's 1665, in Aldgate in the city of London. There is fear all around. The plague is spreading so fast and no one knows how it leaps from person to person. I was all right for a while, but then one of my family got it, and now we've been boarded up in the house, forbidden to go outside. Left to die. They leave food at the door sometimes, but not enough, and what we really need is water, of which they leave precious little. It's awful in here. Five of us in two rooms, and the air reeking with the smell of my aunt Jane, my mother's sister, as she gets sicker and sicker. The first sign we had was when she vomited two nights ago. I think she had other symptoms but had managed to hide them. But this vile substance that gushes uncontrollably from her mouth cannot be hidden. We sit and watch each other, waiting for the next person to start vomiting. By now Aunt Jane is out of this fearful place, for her fever is such that she has no idea what's going on. Who will be next? Me? My dear mother? Little Jack, no more than a baby? The fear is relentless. Every cough or mutter brings anxious glances. This is truly a terrible time to live.

Prior to her regression, Gill's worst problem was that she wasn't able to care for her new baby properly. Like a lot of babies, little Jemma was sometimes subject to vomiting, and Gill lived in fear that her phobia might one day cause her to drop the baby, as a person being sick could sometimes reduce her to a wobbly wreck, unable to stand. After the regression she was able to rationalize her fear, and because she'd taken notice of her Soul Angel's nudges, she no longer needed them, so her fear went away and she was able to be a good mum to her baby.

Tracey from Aberdeen sent me a heartfelt plea for help that I couldn't ignore. She had phobias, but as they hadn't triggered the result her Soul Angel had intended, the nudges became more forceful and her problems had escalated. She had panic attacks, but it was her constant feeling of isolation that was really getting her down. Her phobias, which were a bit unusual, were being afraid of the wind and having trouble swallowing. All her problems seemed to be linked to her feeling of being unimportant, invisible and vulnerable.

I'm a female, alone, riding in the Sahara Desert. There's just sand, lots of sand, and the sun's very bright. I feel at home here, with no anxieties. My horse is an Arabian, and I feel like I belong with it. I'm wearing a long gown, like a white dress, but I can't see my feet, and I have a yashmak [a veil] over my head and across my face. I've got dark skin and long dark hair that's hidden away under the veil. My name's Satcha and I feel safe on my own, just wandering. There's a palace, and that's where I've come from. I didn't feel safe there, and I don't want to go back. I'm free out in the open. The sun's pleasant and it's very calm, but I have to go back sometime.

I'm going back now. My left arm's sore where my father hurt me. I'm used to that sort of abuse. Some part of me is always hurting.

Now I'm by myself in the palace, but I can hear shouting outside. People are running about, screaming, and I'm watching them from the doorway. It's like they're running past but don't see me. I feel like I could walk past and no one would see me. I'm safe when no one can see me.

Next Life

I'm in a wagon on the American prairies. It's the 1800s. I'm a man in my twenties. I feel sleepy like it's a soothing rocking. We've been on a long journey.

Later

My heart's beating really fast. My throat feels dry. There's a gang of six men laughing and jeering. They've seen me and suddenly I'm in the middle of it. If only they hadn't noticed me! They're beating me and dragging me away. I'm almost unconscious, all floppy and my face is all bruised. They're pulling me towards the tree. They're laughing and putting the rope around my neck! Now I'm outside my body, just watching. I feel very sad like I want to cry, while they're laughing and joking. I'm just so sad. My throat's feeling totally relaxed now, and I'm floating away.

Next Life

I'm a white man. I'm scared of a tornado that's coming my way. I'm in a little town in America, with little cow-sheds and stuff. I'm underground in a bunker looking out. The sky's pitch black and I can see the tornado coming.

*I'm just watching. I think that there are others around, but
I can't see them – all I can see is this black sky. It doesn't
seem to be moving. Nothing's happening. I think that I'm
still inside but it seems like the whole picture has frozen
in time!*

*It's like there's just this one house, my house, and
the tornado hasn't touched it yet. I'm not close to it but
it doesn't seem to be moving. I feel very calm all of a
sudden. The tornado is frozen; it's just hanging over me.*

The therapist took Tracey through a healing process, and
immediately after the session Tracey reported feeling
much calmer. She remembered that sometimes when she
was trying to swallow she saw a man's face, and the rope.

THESE ARE A FEW OF MY FAVOURITE THINGS

Past-life nudges are not always unpleasant. Sometimes
they're just odd, as when people find they're obsessed
with certain things. This phenomenon is called 'gathering
the familiar', and it simply means that we can feel more
comfortable when surrounded by artefacts that hail from
the era of a past life, usually a pleasant one. For instance,
a person might collect objects from Victorian times, or
from the American Civil War, and feel really content when
surrounded by them. Just look at the number of 'collectors'

there are out there. People will go to enormous lengths to obtain a missing piece for their collection, whereas to most people these objects are passing curiosities at most.

Or people sometimes favour a certain style of dress that is reminiscent of a bygone age. This can also happen with places, and explains why people sometimes feel really 'at home' in a certain place, maybe even feel compelled to move there, even though it makes no sense regarding their career, family or finances. These things are not 'wrong' as such, and so long as they don't take you off track from where you're meant to be they can even be helpful. But they should be investigated – people should seek out past-life information, because, after all, that's what your Soul Angel wants you to do – so therefore that's what *you* want you to do.

Once the past life has been recalled and accepted, then feng shui can help people in the final resolution of this. Clearing the clutter can have a double effect, clearing blockages of both your home and your soul by shedding the need to keep these things close by – after all, they were really just a reminder of who you really are, and once you know that you'll no longer need the props.

NIGHTMARES AND DREAMS

Because when we're asleep our brainwaves are more receptive to angelic vibrations, it's no surprise that the dream-state is used to give us spiritual nudges. There are ways to tell the difference between ordinary dreams and those that are really memory snapshots. Dreams that are commonplace easily fade after we awaken. Even nightmares that elicit strong emotions, such as terror or emotional trauma, don't stand the test of time. Even a really scary nightmare won't create the same fear when looked at in the light of day. If you have a recurrent nightmare or dream that not only brings a very strong emotional response while you're having it, but also has an emotional impact that endures, the chances are this was no ordinary nocturnal ramble. In other words, if recalling the circumstances of the dream or nightmare, days, weeks and even years later, still triggers the feelings you had when you were having it, then I'd be fairly certain that it was in fact a past-life memory.

Jessica from London was having really bad dreams for years. They'd started when she was 17 years old, and by the time we spoke had been ongoing for four years. In her dream she was being murdered. It was very frightening as she could see the man who killed her very clearly, and remembered every detail when she woke up. The man had in part strangled her and finally cut her throat. She told me she could feel the hot blood streaming down the front of her neck hours after she woke up. Under hypnosis she recalled the actual incident:

My name is Ella Thomas and I live in an inn in Cornwall. At night I am free and my parents have no idea what I get up to. I discovered a way out onto the roof, from where I can spy on the townsfolk without them knowing I'm there. As I get older, I get bolder, and I stay out there longer.

When I was on the roof I found out that the baker's wife was cuckolding her husband with the farmer from Hookey Lane. It was so funny listening to them kiss and cuddle below me, thinking their secret was safe in the dark. When I was 17 my fun stopped quite suddenly and brutally. That night I heard some men grunting and cursing as they pushed a barrow up the hill. I never knew what it contained. If I had, then maybe I would have hidden away and I wouldn't have been murdered. They were swearing so much that it made me giggle, and this gave me away. I heard a shout as one of their number looked up and saw me peeping over the edge of the roof. I darted back, but not before they saw me. For a few days I kept out of sight, praying that they wouldn't take any action against me. But then one night as I lay asleep in my bed, they sent someone for me.

I awoke with a start as a smelly hand pressed against my mouth and I was lifted from my bed by a giant of a man. He moved with unreal stealth for his size as he manhandled me out of the window. He then dropped me from the roof so that I thought I was ready to die, but before I could even scream I was caught by another pair of arms. The first man dropped to the ground, and my two assailants held me down and tied and gagged me. A sack was put over my head and I was half-throttled by a pair of hands, and I couldn't breathe, so I soon swooned away.

I woke lying on hard, cold ground, still bound and still with the sack stopping me from seeing where I was. Suddenly the moonlight flooded my eyes as the sack was yanked off, and I saw the blade in front of me, held aloft by my abductor. Despite the gag I tried to scream and the man dragged the knife across my neck.

The icy cold feel was soon replaced by heat and I felt my life's blood gushing down my front. The man's eyes met mine and I saw no pity there as darkness took me.

As with the trauma of all violent deaths, Jessica needed some healing to remove hers. In later regressions it was discovered that she'd witnessed some smugglers at their work, and so had been killed to assure her silence. Armed with this new knowledge Jessica had no more nightmares. She went on to discover more of her past lives, so satisfying her Soul Angel. It's interesting to note that, as in many cases, her dreams had started at the same age she'd been in the past life when she'd died. Past-life phenomena of all kinds tend to start in your current life at the same age you were when the triggering event actually occurred in your past.

WEIGHT ISSUES

This is one I have come across time and time again. People know that being overweight (or indeed, very underweight) is bad for their health, and they desperately want to change this because, after all, they're not stupid. However, when it comes down to it, resisting that chocolate bar is totally impossible. I've had people tell me, 'It's as if I get taken over.' Well, of course, that's exactly what happens. Their Soul Angel has used this apparent obsession with eating (or in the case of anorexics, to stop eating) as a nudge to remind them of past incarnations.

Paula from Doncaster asked me to do a past-life reading to explain her passion for and overindulgence in food because she was becoming seriously obese with a BMI of 28. She'd tried everything short of stomach surgery, and she really didn't want to take that drastic step until she'd exhausted all other avenues. She'd tried every diet out there, and even her impending marriage and her desire to look conventionally good in a slender white dress, couldn't stop her path to self-destruction. In reading for this woman I had to take into account all the common past-life causes for weight issues.

These include:

- **having been starved in a past life**
- **having starved other people in a past life**
- **punishing oneself because of perceived past-life crimes.**

In Paula's case, though, it was none of the above, but the very common issue of having died a violent death. In past times being killed suddenly, for no apparent reason or for petty theft, wasn't uncommon, nor was violent death in hand-to-hand combat during times of war, and so it had been with Paula. In her past life she had been run through with a sword.

Paula had been a victim of the Wars of the Roses in Great Britain. In 1471 she'd been a soldier in the army of Edward IV, fighting for the county of Yorkshire against that of Lancashire. Although the battle was won, Paula, then in the body known as Jeremy Bead, was killed in a swordfight late in the day. Jeremy was a skinny youth with little flesh on his bones, and he was run through, the sword penetrating his liver and killing him too slowly. He lay on the battlefield in agony for hours. In this lifetime, Paula's subconscious saw a lack of flesh as a danger. She felt that if she'd been fatter as Jeremy, the sword might have missed vital organs and he wouldn't have had to endure a lingering, painful death. Paula's angel had used this pain and fear of blades to nudge her conscious mind into acknowledging the past. In this life Paula felt she was staving off danger to her vital organs by armouring her body with a solid covering of fat. The pain of her death and the fear it engendered totally overran any fear of possibly getting ill through being obese, and so she was unable to use the logical and sensible fear of ill health to overcome her fear of being stabbed.

I normally tell people to go for regression to totally clear this sort of problem, as a psychic reading can only achieve so much. Generally, just having someone tell you about a past-life incident isn't enough – you need to actually re-experience the trauma that started the problem under the guidance of a past-life therapist. However, in Paula's case the upcoming nuptials seemed to give her the extra boost she needed, and Paula was married in a very respectable size-16 dress. I feel, though, that she should go for regression still, to ensure the fear doesn't come back and to continue the path that her Soul Angel obviously feels she should take.

Another person with an eating issue was Jackie of Foyle, and her cause was very similar to the one above, reinforcing the evidence that overeating often has its roots in the past, and can often be traced to a fatal wounding. Jackie is a beautiful person, but it has to be said she would be even more beautiful (and healthier) if she could shed the three stone she constantly lost and regained – and keep it off. Each time she dieted it was getting harder and harder to lose the weight, and finally she decided to look to her past to see if she was self-destructing for some reason or, as I suspected, if she was actually carrying out self-preservation.

My name is Gabrielle and I love to dress and live well. The year is 1924 and everyone I know feels we have to live as much as we can in case war comes to us as again, as we fear it might. I'm American born, and I live in Paris. I have many beautiful gowns and shoes to die for, and I live to the full. Parties go on here night and day, and I love them. The cost of living is cheap here compared to back home and we all make the most of it.

Later

I'm an artist, but independently wealthy. I think I have talent. I hope I have talent, and where else would an aspiring artist live but here in Paris, at this time? A major gallery has optioned my work. I'm so excited! Life is wonderful. The exhibition starts tonight. All my friends

*are coming. This will be the party of the century and the
start of my real life. I never realized how much I wanted
this until I started to believe it could happen. People are
going to adore me, buy my paintings, and commissions
from royalty are likely. I drink a gin and tonic while getting dressed in my most fabulous gown. I look fantastic.
I'm the ideal clothes horse; although some might say I'm a
little bony, the clothes hang on me to perfection. Design-
ers would almost pay me to wear their creations. I've got
a new fur coat so I'm going to walk to the gallery. People
in the streets will see me and wonder who I am. They'll
soon know!*

*Walking was a mistake. I'm scared. Someone is follow-
ing me. I shouldn't have worn my fine clothes and the
jewellery. Why was I so vain? If he wants to rob me he
can. I won't resist. I'm tempted to throw my rings and
necklace onto the ground and run. There's another one!
He's jumped out in front of me. He's got a knife. No! No!
I'll give them my jewels. The knife flashes and I feel nothing at first. Now I feel a pain, hot and deadly. Then I'm
suddenly growing cold, falling, fading …*

Jackie responded to regression very well. 'It was awful,
such a sudden and violent death, and just as the good
things in life were mine for the taking. What rotten

timing! Everything was laid out like a map and then I got stabbed to death. Why couldn't they have just wounded me? Because I was so skinny, that's why! No wonder being skinny doesn't feel "safe" to me.'

The fact that Jackie died so unexpectedly is what has lived on with her. In this life it's holding her back in two ways. First, she's a bit afraid to be happy in case it is suddenly snatched away. Finding out why she fears that will happen should start her towards healing and letting herself live life to the full. Second, her weight is obviously something she wears like armour. She believes that if she's thin a knife will easily pierce vital organs, just like Gabrielle. With all the padding she lays down she thinks maybe she could survive a knife attack. Since understanding that this problem was in the past and not going to happen to her again, she has started to lose weight and keep it off.

REPETITIVE RELATIONSHIP PROBLEMS

So many people spend their whole lives searching in vain for that special someone. You only have to look at most celebrities, who on the face of it have everything the man in the street could dream of – financial security, friends, adulation, property, etc., and yet they are desperately un-happy and lurch from one unsuccessful relationship to another, never finding what they often envy us 'regular' people for having – a dependable, loving partner. Other people repeat destructive cycles over and over, never able to break out of the rut that sees them choosing the wrong partner every time. Still others find it hard to keep friendships going and end up going to the wildest lengths to impress people.

Angela of Wyoming was one such person. She always had an inferiority complex and never felt people really liked her as she was. So she started making up stories to impress people, keep them 'onside' and wanting to be her friend. The lies were always harmless as such, white lies, she thought, just to make her seem more important than she was. But then her fantasy walls started coming down, because people started to find out about her lies. It looked as if her whole world was coming to an end and in desperation to help her stop this destructive habit, she asked me if there was a past life lurking somewhere that could enable her to get herself under control. We decided to opt for a telephone regression, for which I induced a light meditation in her. This was what she discovered, which was later confirmed in a regression with a hypnotherapist.

I am an outcast. A Paraiyar, *unloved and untouchable by my people, the Tamils. My family were once considered high born, people of rank and respected by all, but now we are servile, and looked down upon. I am reincarnated from that time, but it is now the year 1650 and I find it impossible to bear – this new position in society. I died aged 30, I think from a broken heart because I was so unloved. I will never find myself in this position again. On my deathbed I swore to myself that in the next incarnation I would make sure I was important, loved and revered!*

This was a fascinating insight and totally explained why Angela would have felt the need to lie her way into respectability in this life. I feel that her Soul Angel would have tried to talk her out of this course of action, but when that failed it would have taken the drastic action of having Angela's lies revealed, so to push her into taking some remedial action. I suggested that Angela go for past-life regression because I wanted to make sure all feelings of lack of worth from that dreadful past life were totally healed. Angela is now a much happier and more honest person.

This next story involves both relationship issues and mysterious health problems.

Judith from Austin, Texas went to her therapist suffering from seizures and complained of a rocky relationship with a current boyfriend. She decided to look into her past-life memories for the answers. The answers came from three past lifetimes, one in which she knew her current boyfriend. Each of these lifetimes taught her lessons that are valuable in this life.

First Life Recalled

I'm a 20-year-old woman living in a medieval farm community in Spain. I grow herbs and make handcrafted things for the village. My lover is my boyfriend in my current life. He's a knight from a neighbouring village whose men fight often with the townspeople in my village. One day I'm hit on the head by a ball and chain wielded by some savage people from the other village where my lover lives. They kill me because they know of my relationship with the knight.

'The seizures are a result of my emotions surfacing from this lifetime after I met my current boyfriend, because of the head trauma I'd suffered when I died in that past life.'

Second Life Recalled

I'm a woman, a native of Egypt and I work preparing food. In this life my current boyfriend is there again. I love him but he denies his feeling for me. Although I never marry, I live to be in my nineties, and die peacefully.

Third Life Recalled

I'm a Choctaw Native American man living in Utah as a hunter, fisherman and trapper in my tribe. I die from a gunshot wound to my head, inflicted by pioneers who want the land we live on. My father was a wise man in the tribe and I was very close to him in that lifetime.

Judith was one of the lucky ones, as she came out of her session with a clear idea not only of what had caused her health and relationship issues, and the knowledge to stop them, but also knowing her master plan. She was to study the use of herbs for natural healing, and to encourage others to learn to live in harmony with nature.

Another common relationship problem goes like this: You meet someone and feel instantly, 'This is the one!' You feel you know them already, and what, you think, could be a better basis for a long-term, happy relationship than this? After all, people with successful marriages always tell you that it's very important to be friends with your partner as well as lovers. You're very happy, and thinking babies and cottages and happily ever after. It's common in these relationships that both parties feel so committed that they will even start a business together or buy a house in joint names. Sometimes this all goes very smoothly, of course, and their first impression turns out to have been right. But sometimes it doesn't end happily ever after. Sometimes what has happened is that you've recognized this person from a past life, albeit subconsciously. What feels so comfortable isn't deep love – well, not of the partnership kind – but familiarity. Nostalgia from a previous happy time together fools you into thinking this is your soul mate for this lifetime. In these cases what happens next is that a bombshell drops. Soul Angels are giving this person a nudge because they know this partnership isn't the one you contracted to, and that the real McCoy is standing in the wings unable to get close because you're wrapped up in a fantasy situation. So the nudges grow and eventually your partner says they have to leave, but because they're obeying subconscious nudges they can't tell you why. Of course, it could be you that gets the nudges and you that leaves the relationship. Either way, hearts get broken. Until, that is, past-life recall shows you why they or you left, and with understanding come acceptance and a paving of the way for your real soul mate to arrive.

Jordan of Basildon was one such person. Her partner, Graham, left her quite suddenly and could never give her a good reason why. Jordan was heartbroken because she'd been so sure Graham was 'the one'. She couldn't move on until she knew why, and regression showed her the way.

My name is Clarisse and I'm French, aged around 87. I live in Marseille and the year is 1872. I married very young and loved my husband, Claude, very much. There wasn't huge passion, but he kept me safe and I was happy with him. He died about ten years ago, quite suddenly. Recently I was looking through some old chests and I came across some letters that I'd never seen before. I was shocked because the letters were to me, but I'd never received them. They were from Philippe, my first boyfriend. Philippe and I had the passion that was lacking between me and Claude. When he was killed I had been devastated, and only Claude's love for me had kept me going. But as I read the letters I became horrified, because Philippe had not been dead after all. He'd written me many letters to tell me this and to declare his love for me, but Claude had hidden them. I felt so betrayed, and now at my age there's nothing I can do. I just see that I may have missed out on the life of my dreams with my real, only love.

Jordan was emotional when she came out of regression, but happy, because she'd recognized Claude as Graham in this life. So now his reasons for leaving became clear. Someday, somewhere, Jordan was going to meet 'Philippe' again, and Graham was being moved out of the way so that this time things would go right for them, and he wouldn't stand between them as he once had.

Another example of a relationship from a past life spilling over into a current one, and in this case actually causing a physical manifestation to prove the deep connection, was this one from Joyce of York. Joyce was a sales account manager, and was very successful. One day a strange man walked into her office, and there was an instant connection between them, and a deep feeling in Joyce that she knew him, although they'd never met before. She didn't know who he was in this life, but over a period of a few weeks during his occasional visits to the office she discovered he was the company chairman. The company was a household name, known internationally. It appeared that he, then, was the most unlikely candidate to be interested in past-life regression.

She started to look out for his visits and ensure she was in the office when he called. Their meetings were professional at all times, until, that is, they got talking after a meeting one day. They both agreed that there was 'something', they could not decide what, that connected them, and they got to talking about the possibility of past lives.

A deeper relationship formed that was electric beyond words, a bringing together of two souls, and eventually Joyce started asking more questions. She wondered if it could it be that they'd been together in a former life.

Joyce went for past-life regression to see if she could find out. She told him she was going to try it and he asked her to report back on what had happened. Could they have been together before? The first session left her in tears, because she couldn't find a life where they had been together. Her anticipation was so strong, and she thought that maybe she wanted it so much that she was trying too hard.

She tried again, remaining calm.

> *I'm standing on the shores of Atlantis, watching the sea, waiting for my lover, who went to sea to rescue some fellow Atlanteans. I wait on the shore for a long time, never moving away in case I should miss his appearance on the horizon. My anticipation is enormous, and I am so agitated and tense, but I know he will return. When his ship comes into view the elation is overwhelming. As I hold him in my arms both of us have tears streaming down our faces. I'd known he would return. I'd had faith where others had doubted. He is my first-ever love, the first man I have ever known sexually, in any lifetime. He is the one to whom I gave my virginity all that time ago. As I look into his eyes I recognize him as the chairman.*

After the session Joyce mentioned that every time she came into contact with the chairman in this life, she would bleed vaginally. She could not explain this at all. Her doctor couldn't explain the erratic bleeding, nor could a consultant. Joyce put this down to the chairman being her first-ever true physical love, a love so deep it manifested in her body, which enacted losing her virginity every time she met him in this life.

Mary, of Ruislip, wanted to have a past-life regression because she was feeling depressed and wanted to understand why she had such a strong fear of intimacy with men. She'd read Brian Weiss's books on past-life regression, which had helped her begin to realize that this fear may have originated in a past life. Mary was aged 35 and had never been married, had never had children, and hadn't had a serious relationship or experienced sexual intercourse. Originally she thought this was because she hadn't met the right man yet, but deep down she felt there might be something wrong with her. She'd come close to having sex a couple of times, but there had always been a reason or excuse not to, so it hadn't happened.

Mary worked as a scientist in the medical profession, and although she had a very logical, scientific mind, she was also very sensitive. Her therapist was concerned that Mary's fear of intimacy might have originated in her childhood, but she was assured that Mary had no memory of any sexual abuse. She said her childhood was fine and that she had a twin sister who was married with children. Her therapist nonetheless gained permission to take Mary back through her childhood, just to be on the safe side. Mary was happy to do this as she really wanted to understand as much as she could about herself. She couldn't remember much about her childhood, and had a blank spot.

I'm aged six, sitting in my living room at home, playing with my Barbie dolls. I feel ashamed and bad because it's bad to undress my dolls. Mum said it's bad.

I'm aged three, playing in my bedroom with my dolls. My mum comes in and says, 'Don't do that, it's rude.' I'd been simulating sex with my dolls, pretending that Ken and Barbie were having sex.

('My therapist thought this play-acting was a bit unusual for a three-year-old and so she asked me to go back to the first time I had thought about sex.')

I'm a young girl aged 15, called Missy. I'm on a wooden Spanish sailing ship, on the way to England. The time is the 1700s.

I'm in the galley of the ship, serving three scruffy-looking sailors, who looked like pirates. *('My therapist told me later that my voice changed dramatically to fearful as I described one of these pirates as having a dark beard and said that he reminded me of my grandfather Fred in my present life.')*

I'm an orphan because my parents were stabbed to death by a beggar with a knife while they were walking along the street. My younger brother and I escaped, but he ran away and I never saw him again. I had nowhere to go and so I lived on the streets while I searched for my brother, ending up at the wharf. The sailors took me onto the boat and tricked me into going with them, saying they would help me find my brother.

My name is really Francine, but the sailors call me Missy. The sailor with the beard regularly takes me to his cabin and rapes me. I'm extremely upset and angry at what happens to me. He is ugly. His beard is scratchy and itchy. I hate men and I'm scared of them. ('This is where I made the vow that was to be carried with me beyond death.')

I was killed when other pirates invaded the ship and I was shot with a spear, which pierced my shoulder so that I bled to death.

A Later Life

I'm a woman called Magdalene and I'm 23. I have long brown hair and I'm wearing a purple robe. I live in a castle in the 1800s, with an old man who is very wise. He wears long robes and looks like a wizard. He is helping me to make potions so that I can heal people. I was born in a cottage on the edge of a forest. My mother had died many years previously, and I lived there with my father, who became sick. I tried to heal him with my potions. I regularly went to a local market to sell my healing potions. However, the villagers thought I was a witch and wouldn't buy them. My father was an angry man, and when he'd been well he had regularly beaten and raped me. My brother had run away in fear of our father. When Father died I went to live in the castle with the wizard.

Now I'm 85 and my brother is by my side as I'm dying. The wizard has left me the castle, and my brother has come back to care for me. As I die and leave my body I begin to understand the connection between my two lives as Missy and Magdalene, and my current life as Mary. I can see a strong theme running through them, and I begin to understand my life lessons. As Mary I carry feelings of shame from my past lives as Missy and Magdalene. This combined with the feelings of fear of men and sex and my vow to hate men, has prevented me from experiencing a true intimate and loving relationship in my current life.

As I floated over Magdalene's body, I could see a beautiful white being, who came close to me and spoke telepathically to me. This was my spirit guide, Rae, who said, 'Don't worry, child. You will be OK. You are safe now and there will be a man for you in your life very soon.' The *lesson I have to learn is to trust, to begin to trust people, and myself.*

After the session Mary was elated, and very surprised at where her fear had come from. She felt more motivated and self-confident about meeting men, and admitted she had always wanted to study energy healing. She was now looking forward to the future.

UNRESOLVED PAIN

People sometimes have pain that modern medicine can't find a cause for. No number of tests or medications seem to be able to resolve it, and this can often be a past-life nudge. It turns out that the person may have received a traumatic injury in their past life, possibly a fatal one, and this depth of pain and fear from that moment keeps the emotional memory floating near enough to the surface of the subconscious that the person's Soul Angel can give it a prod.

Jason from Harwich was one such person. He'd suffered from stomach cramps for years, and he'd been tested, he said, for almost every disease known to man in an attempt to find the cause. He'd changed his diet and ingested huge amounts of antacids, all to no avail. It took a journey into his past life to resolve the problem.

It's Victorian times. Don't ask me the year as I know nothing of such things. I'm a bit ragged, my clothes are torn and dirty and my shoes have holes in them. But I have a happy if poor life. I have a wife, Jenny, and a small son, and my only real worries are keeping a roof over our heads and feeding us all. My family is everything to me. I'm in the park today, walking across the grass towards some metal railings and a gateway. I'm happy, excited, because I have a good chance of gaining a position in a big house with a rich family. The job comes with servant's quarters, and so my wife and son will be able to move out of our rough home and into a clean place with plenty of spare food in the kitchen.

As I emerge into the street I can see the house I'm going to, in its prestigious position right next to the park. This is a busy street, thronging with horses and carriages. I start across the road. Suddenly I hear shouting, screaming and clattering. A carriage comes flying down the street with no one in the driver's seat. I don't know what's happened but I can see tragedy unfolding. A woman is pushing a perambulator across the cobbles. She's right in the path of the runaway carriage and within seconds she'll be crushed under the hooves and wheels. I can't stop myself; I rush towards her. I'm almost upon her and the horses are almost upon her, too. I reach out but I know there isn't time to push her to safety.

Then the lead horse throws up its head. It sees the woman and the pram. It swerves. For whatever reason it's not willing to trample her. I see its nostrils, flaming red inside. I feel its snorting breath and then it's on top of me. I'm pushed to the ground and then the wheels hit me. One of them runs across my stomach.

The pain is indescribable, and as the people gather round me, as well as pain I feel despair. I am to die here in the gutter and Jenny will be left alone. It's all I can think of as the darkness overtakes me.

('Something amazing happened at this moment. I could feel my hopelessness as I passed into a white light, and then my past-life therapist instructed me to remain in the light and look back at the life again.')

I see my body, broken and twisted, but then the picture moves and I see Jenny and my son. Tears are streaming down Jenny's face as she's told of my death. I can feel her fear and grief, but also, as she clutches our son, her terror at what will become of him. Then I hear the man who has come to break the news speaking. He's telling her that he believes my actions saved the life of his little boy and his nanny – the woman in the street. I don't think that's true, but the man continues saying that Jenny can take our son and live out her days as a maid in the man's house, and that she will be cared for, always.

When Jason came out of the hypnosis session he was crying with happiness. Both guilt and trauma had been relieved by his memories and the therapist's instinctual guidance for him to look back to see what had happened following his death. Jason never had the stomach pain again, and he now works with abused children.

There are of course many other signs of past-life trauma – for instance scars, recreated in actuality or with tattoos, apparent 'bad luck', career problems, health issues, a feeling that something is missing, depression, weight problems, phobias, obsessions, compulsions ... the list is endless.

CHAPTER 5

The Past Blocking the Present and Future

Blockages are the most common way that your past can affect your day-to-day life. People feel that they could and should be moving forward to something great and wonderful. How many times do you say or hear someone else say, 'There must be more to life that this'? Or, 'I always thought I was destined to do something special.' Many, many people spend years searching for an elusive 'something' that is going to change things, open doors, make people look up to them – but they never find it. They will often complain that they're being held back, perhaps by family, perhaps by employers or teachers, or lack of time or money, or perhaps by fate in general. What all these people fail to realize is that only one thing is holding them back, and only one person is responsible – themselves. If they refuse to listen to their Soul Angel's nudges about past lives, as most do, they will rarely find the right path by themselves. Their Soul Angel *is* them, in a certain way, and so they are basically not listening to themselves. It's a human characteristic that we don't like to be told what to do – even by ourselves!

The 'blockage' that people perceive is actually caused by them having *soul amnesia*. They have literally forgotten who they are, and regaining past-life memories is the quickest way to get back on track. I'd compare it to someone in this life who gets struck down by amnesia, perhaps in mid-life, perhaps as the result of an accident. It would be almost impossible for them to pick up the threads of their life if they didn't know their own history. If they didn't know who they were, didn't recognize friends and family, didn't have access to all the knowledge and the lessons they'd learned throughout their life, then their whole life would be off track until they got their memories back. Past-life amnesia is just as debilitating when it comes to spiritual development. If you don't know your own history before this lifetime, then you won't remember the conversations with your Soul Angel when it came to deciding on your master plan for this current life. Your past lives are just as important to your spiritual development as what you go through on your journey in *this* life is to your social development.

While triggering past-life memories is not a guarantee of awakening instantly to your master plan and unblocking your progress, it is a *very* big step in the right direction. Gradually, past-life memories will bring you a complete picture of yourself, and the rest is sure to follow. I have to say that I don't know anyone who has recalled every detail of every past life, but most seem to just get enough to make the journey clear and the end-game attainable.

What about the future? Not only can our past-life amnesia block our current lifetime, it can also affect those lives yet to come. Progression (looking into future lives), the opposite of regression (looking into past lives) is quite a new therapy (1960s), but in some cases it can actually unblock present lives as effectively as regression. This is because patterns can be observed and traced backwards into the current life. Changes can then be implemented in the current life, thereby breaking the patterns and changing your future lives.

There are some additional benefits with progression. With regression, the memories revealed can sometimes be verified by historical events, but in my personal experience I've discovered that this rarely proves your beliefs to sceptics. If you can't find recorded physical evidence of your past (which, as in my case, might easily have been obliterated over time), then sceptics will say it isn't true. If recorded physical evidence is found, then they will say that you must have accessed it previously, even if subconsciously. So, you can't win. With progression, so long as the facts of the life are reliably recorded, future actual events can prove that the life the person saw was an actual one, complete with events that eventually came to be. Yet another dimension to this fascinating branch of peering into our own subconscious is that, as with regression (when it's used to look just as far back as your current childhood in order to uncover the roots of problems), progression can also just take visionary steps forward in your current life, which can help you correct any missteps you might be taking today.

Also, as I've said, you can change your reality, your script, and progression is a way for the individual to monitor this. If in past lives you've seen a cycle, a repetitive way of getting things wrong that has made your past lives appear to follow a pattern, creating a rut you've been unable to escape from despite help from your Soul Angel, then after regression you might find things have changed. If you feel you've woken up spiritually, and are perhaps even following the right track this time, then in progression you'll find the cycle has indeed been broken and that future lives have become very different from past ones. If, on the other hand, the cycle seems to continue into future lives, then you'll know you have more work to do.

CHAPTER 6

A Conversation with Your Soul Angel

*Angels must have a sense of humour
or they'd go crazy!*

Not everyone passes their exams the first time around. We all have to progress, stage by stage, and our Soul Angels are there to help and guide us. We can't always succeed in wrapping everything up in one life, sometimes two, or five, or 85 are what it takes to get everything sorted out. We can't be given too much help, just enough to push us along in baby steps. Left entirely alone we'd probably never figure it all out and get it right, but also we have to struggle on most of the way, learning by our mistakes and moving on.

I was once challenged by a one-life believer who said that God only gives us one life and that's the only chance we get to get it right. I found this would be an impossible challenge, and I don't think a merciful God would give us impossible challenges. It's said that God never gives us more than we can handle, and giving us one life, to understand everything, to get everything balanced and to emerge victorious (and righteous) just isn't the way the God I feel would behave. I've also said that all people deserve an equal chance to please God, and yet the world isn't an egalitarian place, so one life doesn't offer up the opportunity for balance. A Christian woman questioned this, saying that those who've had an impossible life won't be judged like the rest of us, so they still only need one life. My answer is that everyone deserves the *right to be judged* and have their turn to stand before God as an achiever, so we need many lives in order to experience enough to give us that equal opportunity.

Repeating lives are a real cosmic jigsaw puzzle – confusing, exciting and often confounding – but we will get there in the end. Each and every lifetime, when viewed from an objective perspective, can be seen to lead clearly onto the next. We get some things right and some things wrong, but slowly, bit by bit, the pieces fit together and make a whole picture.

I often imagine, with a smile, a pair of Soul Angels leaning against a lamp post, discussing their charges. One might say, 'Has yours woken up yet?' and get the reply, 'No, it's like banging your head against a brick wall!'

If you try and imagine that one of this pair is *your* angel – in other words, is *your* divine self discussing *you* – it will probably make you smile, too, when you see how stubborn you're being. It must be so frustrating, for from their perspective everything must look so simple. They can see the history of your lives stretching back across time, from start to finish, and they can see all the progress you've made in lifetimes, as well as all the setbacks. I think the map they can see must look a little like an almost completed game of Snakes and Ladders. All you have to do is throw the right number, go the right way, and up the ladder you'd go to the finish, but instead most likely you're teetering on the head of a snake, considering the downward slide with relish. Our angels must do a lot of groaning in response to our antics.

Once you've left this mortal coil and crossed over, you'll be met by this angel, your Soul Angel, and although it will be possible for you to meld with them, it won't happen right away, because you two will have things to discuss. First will come your realization that you perhaps messed up a few times, and with the divine knowledge that will flood you at this time you'll know the truth of everything you did and how it affected your soul's progress, both positively and negatively. It will be your turn to groan as you realize your missteps and mistakes. Your Soul Angel will comfort you, pointing out that all humans make mistakes and that your divine part, your Soul Angel, is the biggest part of you. Your mistakes are easily diluted in your divine whole, and there should be no guilt to carry forward. Your body may well have been damaged during your lifetime and so you may be carrying some emotional and energetic trauma from those wounds. This pain will be healed by your Soul Angel. From there the two of you will most likely discuss how long you should remain in spirit before you go back to Earth. Perhaps a long rest is needed. All hurt and emotional stress would be absorbed by your Soul Angel and recuperation would start right away, for you would be in the place your soul truly calls home. During this time you will see all that you have ever been and all that you can aspire to be, and see clearly the best route for that to happen. You'll go over the lessons that were put before you in your most recent life, and see how well you did at learning them.

Once this has happened, or if you decide between you that your soul needs to go back to a physical body right away, it's time for some choices. At this point you'll get some more help.

During one of my early deep meditations I found myself before what I called *The Council of 12*. At the time I had no idea really what this meant. I felt a lot of respect for these beings, as well as a large degree of affection. It was perhaps how you might feel standing in front of some of your old schoolteachers – the ones you really admired and whose lessons you really enjoyed. You'd feel a little small and ready to listen to their words. You wouldn't really feel afraid, but you would feel that they deserved your undivided attention and respect. Their words to you, both of praise and possibly of gentle chastisement, would mean everything.

I later learned from my mentor at the time, Sylvia, that this Council of 12 were the Elders I would be brought before to discuss how my next life should go. You and your Soul Angel would talk with the Elders, and of course listen to what they had to say. Then you'd leave there and have a final chat before being reborn.

Some of the topics of discussion would be:

- **Which sex should you be?**

- **What sort of parents should you be born to, to make sure you (and they) are presented with the right lessons, experiences and opportunities?**

- **Whereabouts in the world should you be born?**

- What era should you live in next?

- Which members of your soul group should you re-enact with?

- Which soul mate should be with you in your life in order to progress your soul in the best possible way?

- If you are to have children – who should they be?

- What are the most important lessons for you to learn based on what the Elders have told you?

- Should you be affluent and have an apparently easy life in order that you can perhaps help others?

- Should you be poor and needy?

- Should you have an illness or disability?

- Is there any 'unfinished business' that you need to resolve in your next life?

- Are there any family issues to work through?

- What is your main aim – your master plan – your reason for going back?

As you can see, the whole thing is incredibly complicated, so it's not surprising that we often get some of it wrong. The plan will be totally sound when we create it, because in spirit, with our Soul Angel and the Elders, we'll have access to all the knowledge and experience in the universe. But of course, once we go through the birth trauma and start to have our personality shaped, and of course lose touch with our souls, that's when the trouble starts and the mistakes get made. This is also why we have to come back here many, many times before we can even begin to hold on to our spiritual integrity through all that human life throws at us. And that, as I've said, is the challenge we agree to. We agree to it because our angelic parts know it's the way for us to evolve into the ultimate angel beings.

GENDER

To achieve further balance, another reason we need to live many lives is so we can experience being both genders. People are often staggered to know they were once a member of the opposite sex, but when you think about it this explains why some 'new' (and eminently desirable) men are overtly connected to their feminine side. This is because they've previously experienced being strong and accomplished women, and are all the better for it. These men have obviously reached a point of balance between the two genders. But you also get some men who are very needy and weak, feeling that their partner must be the one to support them emotionally, and often financially too. These men have spent longer as women who existed in eras where they were not emancipated and were treated very much as second-class citizens, or were possibly abused at the hands of a man. They are not in balance and will need a few more lives of highly masculine, or strong female, energy to sort them out. You also get men who seem to have an overload of testosterone and make 'macho' their byword. These are men who in their future will experience many lives as a woman in order to balance their energy.

You also get women who are very feminine and yet also capable of independence and are strong in mind and body. These are souls who have also experienced lives as both genders in balance, and are therefore better equipped to deal with life. On the other hand you get women who have spent most of their previous lives as men. You also get women who, like the needy men, need propping up all the time, because that's what their previous, negative life experiences have imprinted on them. These are women who need to get some of their power back before they can become balanced in gender energy.

If there ever comes a day when all souls are balanced, that will be the day when there is true equality.

Here are some examples of people who can recall living as both genders.

I'm a small boy, which is a strange feeling as in my current life I'm a middle-aged woman. I'm aged about ten years old and the year is somewhere in the 1200s. I'm in a huge kitchen and there's no one else here. There's a big fire with pots hanging over it. Wonderful smells come from the pots and I realize I'm very hungry. My mouth waters as the aromas waft past me. There isn't time, though, to taste what's in the intriguing pots. On the big wooden table there's a hunk of cheese, and that's what I'm after. I grab it and turn to run, but there's a man there. He draws a knife and I start yelling for someone to help me. He's going to kill me for trying to fill my belly. Another man comes in just in the nick of time and he takes hold of me. The first man gets my other arm in his hand and they have a tug of war with me. The second man obviously outranks the first one, who lets go. I'm dragged off down a stone hallway, my feet catching on the floor and the walls as I lose my footing and he hauls me ever faster. He's saying something about my 'stink'. I'm locked in a room and after a while he comes for me again, and again I'm dragged off to God knows where. Another room, a steaming tub and three women! They strip off my clothes, despite my yells to leave me alone, and then I'm lifted aloft and dumped into the hot water. ('It was an extraordinary feeling because I could actually sense my boy genitals shrinking from the heat.')

Later

I'm a squire to the knight who saved me. I'm happy and well-fed, but it doesn't last. One dark night six months later, my knight is slain while he sleeps, and I'm cast out again. At least this time, thanks to him, I have a good start for the rest of my life. I'm strong, not thin, and I feel I'll make my way …

Further case studies show how we often switch genders. This is from a woman's session.

I'm in a desert. There's not much vegetation. It looks like the southwest. I see myself at work there. I'm a potter. I'm in the marketplace. It seems like it is early. I'm a male, maybe 25–30 years old, but I look like I'm 50. Maybe I'm not in the best of health, or I don't feed myself properly. I'm intent on the potter's wheel. People ask me what I sell. I make housewares. If I sell them, OK. If I don't, it's OK. I don't have as many customers as the people who sell vegetables or cloth. I'm intent on the potter's wheel. My hands are dry from the clay. I'm a loner, but I am able to communicate easily. I'm just not one for small talk. I don't seem to live long. When I die, the people miss me, but my passing also hasn't made a great dent in their lives. I simply served a purpose, filled a need.

('My therapist asks me, "What wisdom did you gain from viewing that past life?" I answer, "That you can be content with life. You can be internally happy. He [the potter] didn't care what people thought. He didn't have to impress anyone except with knowledge and skill. He had all that he needed. He was willing to die, and he died quietly." My therapist asks me, "How might that wisdom change what you do with the rest of your life here?" I answer, "It could actually make me more of a loner. I realize now that my interests are sufficient. I don't need to look elsewhere for approval. I can do as I like. Life is too short to be upset about everything. Who knows how long or short it will be?"')

I'm in a hospital. It feels comfortable and familiar, but I don't work there. I see an X-ray machine. I'm getting a treatment. Is it for cancer? I'm not happy but I'm not scared either. I seem to have to do this frequently. In this life I make the most of every day. I don't know how long I will be on Earth. I don't have all the time in the world to be content. I have to find it now.

('I'm asked, "If the aspect of you in that lifetime could give the aspect of you here some advice, what would that be?" I respond, "Don't worry about the future. Enjoy each day, without looking to the future. There might not be one. I will try to be happier like I used to be as the potter. I take life too seriously. The negativity got to me. I internalize too much. I'll stop the negative thoughts. I'll be more positive. I'll let things bounce off me."')

The following story came from a man who was finding it impossible to maintain a viable relationship with a woman. He was to learn a series of lessons from a series of past-life memories.

First Life Recalled

I'm the owner of a cattle ranch and I live a simple but good life, close to nature, in Montana in 1846. I am very much in love with my wife, who is a warm and passionate woman. My wife is a dependable woman, but has never given me a child. She dies young, aged 45, from a chest infection, and I am left alone with no family, until I die in my seventies. I am very lonely for most of my life. ('I recognize that this wife of mine from the 1800s is now someone I know in my current life. She refuses to commit to me in this life, and now I understand that is because she wants more than I've been able to give her in our past life together, even though consciously she doesn't remember us having shared a life together before.')

Second Life Recalled

The year is 1910 and I'm in New York City. I'm a banker. I belong to a church choir and meet a girl there. ('I recognize her as my current-life girlfriend.') *I'm totally obsessed with money, which I thought would bring me happiness, but it hasn't. I should marry my girlfriend, but I never do. My life is filled only with my greed for money, which in the end means nothing. I stay friends with the girl, but we could have had so much more.*

Third Life Recalled

It's France, the 1700s. This time I'm a woman and I marry a man. ('I recognize him as a former girlfriend in my current life who wouldn't commit to me.') *We are happy together. But I die very young. I'm only in my twenties when there's a boating accident. I'm on a freighter crossing to England and it capsizes.* ('I realize that in this life the girl wouldn't commit to me because subconsciously she didn't want to go through the trauma of losing her partner again.')

Another example of how we have to sample experiencing both genders.

First Life Recalled

My name is Matthew and I'm an Englishman. I was born in the mid-1800s and I'm a member of a wealthy family. They have several businesses and a shop. It is a quiet life, with little excitement. Eventually I inherit the shop and the businesses and I run them happily with my wife. We have three children. I love foxhunting and carry on with my life until I succumb to tuberculosis. I die in the very early 1900s.

Next Life Recalled

I'm a dancer, a Middle-Eastern woman with painted toenails and ankle bracelets. I dance in a sheer costume and I live life to the full. Then when I'm 19 years old, war comes to us from a neighbouring kingdom and I am killed.

Next Life Recalled

I'm a man again, a soldier. I'm stationed in a castle in Belgium in the 1600s. I hate fighting and I hate killing, but I have to do it. I have to obey orders. I always knew that I'd die in battle, and I do.

PARENTS

Choosing parents is tricky, and it's a tricky subject to address. Once we're here we sometimes can't imagine any reason why we would have chosen the parents we did. Perhaps we are abused or hurt by them. All I can say is that, whatever happens, there will be a reason for it. Surprisingly, in these cases it's often chosen by us for the parents' souls' sakes. In spirit we may love these particular souls so much that we'll agree to be abused by them in order that they will be changed by the experience. It's pretty much impossible for us to imagine ourselves in that position, of choosing a really awful life (in human terms) for the sake of another's soul, but this is the difference between spirit and human. In spirit, the lives we lead appear very brief and the suffering we may endure will seem insignificant when compared with the gains. It's the long game.

Sometimes our parental choice before life comes back to bite us very quickly and we're in danger of taking a wrong path because of it. In instances like this it's not unknown for a Soul Angel to guide us back to our path with the help of a therapist.

By the time he was 30, Michael, from California, went for regression to try and help him get over his problems. He knew he'd been adopted at birth, and his adoptive parents were lovely people, but that didn't stop him feeling like he had a hole in his heart where his birth mother should have been. He was a very smart man with a good appearance and already had a law degree – however, he was not doing very well in business or with his love life. He felt lonely and disconnected emotionally from people. A lot of therapists take their clients back into their current lifetime first – starting maybe with their teens or younger and then to five years old and then to the day of their birth. Michael was a good subject and trusted his therapist. Once he was experiencing being in the womb he was able to tune his mind in to that of his birth mother. He discovered that she was a teenager at the time and was scared. He felt that she loved him, but she knew she had to allow someone else to be his parents. He was healed and able to bond with her right away, and his heart filled with love for the young, vulnerable girl his mother had been. His therapist was able to say the right words to him, putting a new programme into his mind and dissolving the old programming.

After just a few sessions, Michael's life and affairs were healed. He immediately did very well with his law practice and soon met and married his soul mate, and they went on to have a child.

WHERE WE LIVE

The place we are born may often be dictated by the parents we've chosen. However, sometimes we might go back to a place we've lived before in order to right some wrong or so that it will give us a clue, by its familiarity, of the fact that we've lived before.

THE ERA

There might be a delay of hundreds of years, if we need to live in a certain era in order to experience a certain way of living. For instance, a lot of souls who suffered in the First or Second World War (or indeed other wars) will choose to come back to a time of relative peace, and endeavour to change things. Many people who were peace protestors in the 1960s, for example, have discovered that they once lived through and probably died in the First or Second World War. They come back during that time of a belief in love and peace to try and change the world. Of course, in the long run, all they change is themselves.

WHOM WE KNOW

We almost always come back to meet up with members of our soul group. Between us we'll have signed contracts, pledging to help each other through the next life, although this might not always be in the ways you'd imagine. Sometimes a member of our soul group might agree to be the 'bad guy', if a bad guy is what we've decided we need in order to have a chance to progress or learn a lesson.

WHOM WE LOVE

That brings me back to soul mates, which is another complicated subject. One of the biggest conundrums people come to me with is why their apparent soul mate has broken their heart and left them for no good reason. There can, of course, be many explanations, but the top two are:

1. We were drawn to this soul mate by familiarity and comfort, because subconsciously we remembered a good past life we spent together as partners. What we thought was true and forever was in fact just nostalgia. When this happens the soul mate will receive messages from their Soul Angel, telling them that they must step aside, usually to make way for the soul mate who is meant to be our partner this time. Because they have no good reason that they know of consciously, they won't be able to give us one, and so we feel hurt and confused.

2. The other most common reason is that the heartbreak is a lesson we are meant to learn from, and is something we asked this soul mate to give us, even though we may have no recollection about the contract we have with them.

In either case, we might be one party or the other – the one who leaves, or the one who is left.

YOUR CHILDREN

Your children, if you're to have any, will be chosen by the same criteria used to select your parents. Each and every member of your family will fit together in your cosmic plan, and hopefully, though not always, do what they're meant to, changing themselves and changing you, as they and you were meant to.

STATE OF BEING

Affluence and poverty can obviously create wildly different scenarios for life. This state of living will have been decided purely in order to give us the best chance of fulfilling our master plan, whatever that may be.

HEALTH AND DISEASE

Health and illness will create very different backdrops to the stage of our life. People will sometimes find it very hard to imagine why they might have chosen to suffer a painful illness or be disabled in some way. Like other lessons, these will have been dictated to us *by* us, at a time when we were in spirit and when this human life would have seemed short and infinitely bearable for the benefits it creates. Once here and suffering, however, such a life will of course loom very large in our consciousness and seem interminable. But terminally ill children, for instance, or severely disabled people can be extraordinary examples of courage to others.

They can be a shining light that demonstrates the true way to live. Bearing that in mind, it's perhaps not so difficult to understand how from the point of view of spirit, someone might choose to embrace such a life.

UNFINISHED BUSINESS

Unfinished business might mean many things. The most common is that once in spirit you realize that you failed to fulfil a contract you made with another of your soul group in the previous life, and so you need to interact with them again in order to keep your promise to their soul.

YOUR FAMILY

Family circles are not called that lightly. So often I see people who have gone round and round, life after life, with the same family, playing different roles. Each time they've all committed to get it right next time, heal rifts, understand each other and fulfil any contracts they've made. Sometimes these contracts work out beautifully, and loving family members are reunited.

Peter from Birmingham tells his story:

> It's the 20th century, and I'm a white male aged 15 years, called Albert. I'm in a field, lying down, and I can feel that my leg's broken. The noise is horrendous as a battle rages

around me. I'm wearing boots and brown trousers and everyone around me is wearing the same uniform. There are blasted trees all around and holes in the ground. I'm in one of the holes. My brother is lying dead beside me. It's Connaught, Connaught's my older brother. We were both in the British army. I'm so afraid.

Later

It's dark, I'm not here.

('I was returned by the therapist to the battle scene.')

I was shot in the stomach.

It wasn't right, I shouldn't have been there. I wasn't aware. My death was just like the lights going out, and it went dark. I felt such great love for my brother, knowing we died together and that we'll always be together.

'After the hypnosis I was very emotional. I could feel the pain in my stomach where I was shot. I could smell the place and hear the noise of the battle. In my current life, I was adopted and only found my blood family five years ago. I was reunited with a brother and a sister. I feel very close to my brother, as though we've never been apart. I trust my brother with my life. I recognized my brother in my current life as Connaught, from a photograph of my great-uncle Connaught, who actually died in the battle of the Somme, which is where I believe this memory comes from. Although I was very emotional after the session, it was the happiest day of my life, as I now understand the closeness I feel for my brother, and I've realized that not even death can part us.'

Because of the complicated dynamics that abound within such groups, and because it only needs one person to miss their spot, not surprisingly the best laid plans, as they say, often go astray. It's a difficult one to sort out, because quite often it's only one or two members of the family who have retained a close enough connection to their souls, or have reunited with their souls, to be open enough to seek the right kind of help.

One example of how this works is apparent in the following regression, where the same two people interact through several lives until finally it all makes sense to them.

First Recalled Life

There's a woman, she's old and sick. She's cantankerous and often nasty, but she's my mother and I do love her. I'm living in a Scandinavian village several centuries ago. The houses are round and small. Plague has struck us and the village is to be abandoned. This old woman is the bane of my life. ('I recognize that in my current life she is my sister, whom I don't get along with. No one gets along with her, not really. She's too hard to please, just like the old woman I see now.') *She's refusing to leave. She's the only one. The wagons are loaded, the horses are hitched and we have to go. We'll be left if we don't go. I'm between a rock and a hard place. If I stay we'll both die, and so will the child inside me. I have no husband any more, and all I have is this wicked old woman. Half-deranged, she screams at me to leave her alone. I've tried everything to persuade her to go, but she won't. If I leave her she'll die, possibly slowly by starvation, or maybe quickly through the plague, and she'll die alone. If I stay we'll die together, or one will go first and the other will die alone.*

'Get away!' she screams. I can't remember the last time I had a soft word from her. She screams at me again. Very well, I decide. I will go. I run out of the house in time to jump aboard the last wagon as it moves away. She's standing at the door. 'Come!' I call to her, holding out my arms. She grimaces, spits on the ground and turns back inside the house. The wagons move off, the sound of hooves competing with the creaking of the laden wagons as they groan beneath their weight …

Second Life Recalled

I'm a young woman who used to be happy. This is England in the early 1600s. My father has recently remarried. ('I know at this point that my stepmother is my current sister. She is also my mother from the previous life.') *My step-mother is so mean that I find it hard to do my duty and love her for my father's sake. When I meet the man I love, my soul mate, she will not allow it. She tries to chase him away, but he will not leave me. We have two happy years together and then she strikes the cruellest blow. One day he is just gone. I know she's to blame but she won't admit it. She won't confess, won't tell me what befell him.* ('I realize this is her vindictive revenge for my leaving her when she was my true mother in the previous life, but I had no choice! Still she blames me.') *Unable to stand life without my love I jump into the sea from a high cliff ...*

Third Life Recalled

I'm a Victorian woman. I'm expecting a baby and I'm ter-rified. I'm sure I'll die in childbirth. I can feel the baby moving within me and I have no idea how it will come out of my body. I've heard stories, each one more terrifying or ridiculous than the last, about how babies are born. I quake with fear at which may be right. I know there will be pain and blood, as I recall my mother giving birth. I wasn't allowed into that room, but I caught glimpses when the door was opened of blood-soaked sheets, and I heard my mother screaming in agony. She never came

*out of that room alive. A small writhing bundle came out
and was taken to the wet-nurse. My mother emerged later
wrapped in a blanket and silent, unmoving. Is that what
will happen to me?*

*Eventually the pain starts and I find myself screaming
on a bed of pain, bleeding, afraid. Then I hear a voice saying, 'It's her or the baby.'*

*For one second I want to cry out for them to save me,
but I find myself sobbing, 'It's her turn. Save her.'*

*Everything fades away and I emerge into a light. I
know that I gave my life for my baby, and I hope that she,
who is to be my sister in the next life, will be grateful and
finally forgive me for once abandoning her in the disease-
infected village two lives ago, and the wicked cycle we've
been on will cease and give us both peace.*

In this case the progression is clear, with one person
perhaps being at fault for abandoning her mother, but the
mother was impossible. In the next life revenge is sought
by the mother. In the next life the first person gives her life
for her baby, to make up for the abandonment that started
all the trouble. But what is happening in the current life
is that the sister, who was the original mother, refuses to
understand the cycle, and is just as nasty and vindictive
as ever. Perhaps subconsciously she now even blames her

sister for abandoning her as a baby. Whatever the reason, the two sisters are only going to continue hurting each other, so one walks away from the other. In this case it is the only way to stop the rot from festering on. In this case no number of lives together are going to heal things, unless the vengeful sister comes to remember and understand the past, but she won't heed the nudges of her Soul Angel, and remains miserable and cruel. So they have to part, and in this case that is the right resolution. The vengeful sister needs many more lives and many more nudges before she is progressed enough to change. Her soul is stagnant, stuck in a rut, and she'd only hold her sister up for many more lives if her sister hadn't woken up and remembered what had started it all.

MASTER PLAN

The most important thing, of course, is to decide on your master plan, that path you should walk through your next life to fulfil your needs and those of your soul. It can be something earth-shaking or something that seems trivial and personal. Either way, every step you take in the right direction, once you're here, is a step towards true happiness.

This is an example of someone who has undergone life-between-lives therapy. Having had several regressions that indicated a repetitive, destructive cycle, and feeling, despite this knowledge, that she was heading for the same painful scenario in this life, Susan of Axminster decided to see if she could discover the conversation she'd had with her Soul Angel prior to this current life. She was hoping to find out if she was in fact meant to go through the same scenario or if she'd just lost her way again in this life as she had in the others. In past lives she'd always fallen out with her children. They'd ended up moving to other countries and taking her grandchildren, and hopes of grandchildren, with them. She felt that was likely to happen to her again, so I took her into that secret realm to see if we could resolve things for her.

These sessions begin like any other, as the person is taken back to the point of their death in the most recent lifetime. They are taken into the light and then look back over their death, before moving ahead into the depths of the light. Then they're asked what they can see there.

I'm surrounded by a beautiful violet light and there's a being inside the light. I can't see any details, but I feel loved and peaceful and serene. I'm going into the light and I can hear the being's voice. It's gentle, tinkling, sort of how I'd expect a benevolent alien to sound, like silver bells. The being is welcoming me back into spirit, and inviting me to review the events of my previous life. I'm encouraged to comment and state my feelings. My body has vaporized and I feel incredibly light. I'm almost floating, and as I am drawn into conversation with the being I am also gradually becoming one with it.

It's very strange, this feeling of having a conversation with yourself, and after a few moments it's like we're speaking with one voice, not even out loud. I think it's just thought forms being exchanged. I see how my family thought of me in that past life. I had thought I was being a caring, loving parent, always worrying, but naturally, about my children. I see that in a lifetime many lives ago, before I had my current problems with them, I lost all of my children to a house fire. Further back I lost my children to an attack on our village. Now I can recall those times I come to understand why I have been perhaps overprotective of my children.

I'm shown my children from the life to come (her present life) and I see myself acting the same way as I have before. Suddenly I see the truth. My previous children and my children to come don't/won't see me as I think I am. They don't see love and concern, they see controlling behaviour and overbearing criticism. They don't see a parent who loves them obsessively; they see a parent trying to live through them, trying to dictate their lives to them.

I'm devastated as I realize at last that I have been repeating this behaviour life after life, terrified that I would lose my children again, and in the end actually creating that loss by driving them away. I understand, though, that this time it's not too late. There's still time for me to change the way I am. With this new wisdom I can help myself.

It was obvious that Susan had come back to her current lifetime in order to try for yet another time to 'get it right' and not make the same mistakes. It was quite difficult for Susan to detach herself from her angel – she said while she was united she felt so wise and so able to understand what she had to do. She was afraid that by detaching she'd lose all of it and go back to being the way she'd been before. But I explained that that wouldn't happen. I had instructed her subconscious to remember everything. She felt very excited when she came out, although a little anxious that she might not be able to 'get it right'. I told her she was now capable of being her own director, with the wisdom to make the right decisions.

Two weeks later Susan told me that, although she was still having to remind herself not to nag, not to question and to loosen her reins on her kids, she was making great strides, and her youngest daughter was actually starting to confide in her mum instead of keeping everything to herself for fear that her mum would interfere. If not for her conversation with her angelic self, I believe Susan would have put herself right back in that vicious cycle she was trying to escape from.

Here is another example of how it can be necessary for a therapist to take you in-between your lives, so that your Soul Angel can help you further.

Jacqueline had had several hypnosis sessions on a number of issues. At the beginning of this particular appointment she was in tears, and feeling a failure. It seemed as if her whole business world was falling apart. Some of her office staff were leaving. She had just experienced a series of false accusations from others she had had business relationships with, and business clients were getting wind of these accusations and deciding not to engage further in any business arrangements. She said that it seemed as if her 'whole world was falling apart' around her. Her attempts at bringing control into this chaotic situation were not working. Her sense of authority and being in charge of her immediate environment was dissolving, and her belief that she was a failure now dominated her perception of herself.

I arrive in what looks like a temple, with polished marble floors. I am a young boy of eight. I am struggling with my studies, learning to be a priest. My mother was a priestess.

She was tall, beautiful, very distant, and wore long gowns made of gold and silk. There was a protocol that I had to adhere to with her: I was her son but only in birth; I was a child of the state. I belonged to the priesthood and was heir to leadership that the priesthood carried in that world. I did not like being in this position. I privately wanted to experience God. I felt a tragic personal failure that I had not found Him as yet.

('My therapist has me go back earlier in that life to another significant event.') *I am three. I feel myself trying to show love to my mother, but she punishes me when I exhibit any such feelings. The world we are in teaches us all to utilize and develop only our minds, and to deny our feelings. As I feel this punishment as rejection by my mother, I begin to shut down emotionally and seek to conform to the development of mental powers. In that I might be accepted.*

('Then my therapist has me regress back further, to experience myself within my mother's womb.') *Here too, I feel the void of connection with my mother. She has shut down emotionally and cannot relate to me. There is no love, no welcoming. I feel very lonely, and frightened. This leaves a major imprint upon my life.*

('Then I am led to other significant events in that life.') *As a young adult I continue my studies but any memories* of feelings or yearnings for God have long since been buried. I've learned to move stone with my thoughts, to control the minds of others, and to rule with what seems a total control over my environment and the physical world. There are also many deep initiations and rituals that are passed on to me in order to provide for the people and the country. I become a priest.

Later in life, as a high priest, I have great responsibility but have grown arrogant about my powers. I am fully ingrained in my position and in charge of all. While we have felt the earth quake and rumble over some years, I've stubbornly believed I could handle (control) any physical disruption.

One afternoon, without warning, the earth begins to move violently. Building walls begin to fall and the marble temples begin to crumble. Fires come up from below, people are falling from buildings into what looks like hell, and they are all dying. I am beside myself. After so many years of the illusion that I have total control of the environment and the world, I do not seem to have control now. I dig deep within my powers but to no avail. I bellow with every ounce of my power. I stand on top of a hill overlooking my city, watching its total destruction. Then I too die in the destruction of the earth's trembling and fire. But I do not leave the earth plane for some time. I cannot comprehend that my world has been devoured by the very earth that I once manoeuvred with my power and control. Soon I realize I no longer have my physical body, and I become full of despair. I wander about the destruction for what seems like a long time: dead tree trunks, smouldering earth, a total devastation of everything I have known. I feel I have completely failed … as a priest, as a leader, as a man and as a soul.

An angel finally appears and takes me. Yet I feel I am unreachable. I am in total collapse. I later find myself in the place where one discusses and reviews one's life. I cannot speak to the celestial being that has been sent to help me. I am stubbornly inconsolable. I am finally taken away to where one has time to heal.

Then, continuing in this 'interlife' and with my therapist's suggestion, I slowly find myself opening to presence of the light of God. The experience begins to soften my stubbornness and melt my self-pity, and I see my own arrogance and how I had shut down emotionally in that life and how the false sense of power over my world had been created in me to replace the loss of love.

I stay in this presence as my heart continues to heal, and then upon my therapist's suggestion, we carry back the presence and the feeling of the light into the major experiences just visited in that lifetime, to watch and feel its impact.

First, in the womb, the presence of the light makes me feel loved from the inside out. While my mother is still distant, I no longer take it personally.

Growing up I feel and see how the presence of the light has an impact on every aspect of my life. I can feel the presence of God, and my development into the priesthood is more whole. I grow as a loving person, not one dominating everything with a misplaced sense of power. I feel humility in the presence of the earth and with others. When the earthquakes happen, I no longer feel the responsibility, or the failure as before. Instead, I know warmth and inner glowing and a sense of the impermanence of things of this world, and how this reflects what is happening inside us.

'I return to this life with a wonderful feeling of gratefulness in my heart. In my work, relationships begin to shift and take on a warmer quality. I find myself less arrogant and controlling and demanding of others. The business begins to take on a more vibrant quality. This session and further regression therapy have yielded a whole different way of being connected inside and growing in the feeling of the awareness of God.'

CHAPTER 7

True Stories of Past-life Healing

During my time as a past-life therapist and columnist I've come across a great many cases of past-life regression where the therapy has opened up a whole new way of living for someone. It's quite extraordinary when you see for yourself the healing that can take place once past lives are revealed and healed. It's very important to select the best person to help you through this if you want to find out who you really are, and there is a lot more information about this later in this book. For now I'd like to show you some examples of the wonders I have seen, and how they go to prove that, while some past-life nudges from our Soul Angels may seen a little harsh or even downright cruel at times, deep down they are all in our own best interests. The people featured here will, I'm sure, go on to discover more and more about their own souls, now that a chink in their modern-day armour has opened, and will at some point recall their plan for being in this world this time.

Sometimes the nudges are a little vague and hard to interpret, but so long as we finally get the message, all can turn out well in the end – except in some cases, as in this first one, where some family skeletons were unearthed. For this reason, some of the names and details have been changed in the following accounts.

'I had lived for some years with a vague sense of dread. It never really formed itself into anything I could grasp, and so of course it wasn't anything I could really seek any conventional help with. I decided to go for hypnosis to see if anything could be found to explain it, but I ended up going further back into my own history than I had thought. I went right back to a past life.'

I find myself lost in a mist. I am a young girl, aged about eight. I feel as though I am dead. I am very cold. ('The therapist directs me back further still.') *I find myself sitting under a large tree. Ahead of me are some cottages. I know I live there, but I don't want to, or can't, go home. I am asked to describe my home nevertheless, and I am able to do so, talking of the stairs being in the kitchen and old-*

fashioned latches on the doors. I also know that my dad has gone off to war and I haven't seen him since. Because of the type of cars I can see I know it must be during the First World War

I give my reason for not wanting to go home as being because I am afraid of a man who lives in our house. I've run away to escape him.

'It turns out after further questioning by the therapist that I died out there under the tree, from cold. Although this was a very sad journey for me to remember, I came out of the session feeling as if something in me had been released, and I didn't have that nameless dread any more. I think the dread had come through to this life with me because I was always afraid of that man in the past. For him to make me leave home and die rather than face him, it must have been something really nasty.

'The most amazing thing was that when I played the DVD of the session to my mum, it made her go very pale, and she told me that I'd recalled the whole story of a family skeleton – which was never talked about – of a family member who had lived in those circumstances and had died of hypothermia. The child's father had died in the Great War and the mother had ended up sharing her home with a very undesirable man who had maltreated the girl when the mother was absent. This was the first

time that my mother had spoken of it and the story was
known only to her, as other family members had passed it
on a long time previously.'

It might seem unusual that someone would come back
into the same family in a new life, but it isn't. Family
circles really do often go round and round like this. More
often the members come back together to try and resolve
something that happened in the past. In fact it's very
likely that this 'bad man' is also back in the same social
circle, if not in the actual family itself, and his presence,
even if he were a woman this time, would stir enough
of this person's past-life unconscious memories to create
that feeling of dread, even though he was not consciously
recognized. There will be opportunities during this lifetime for that past-life dynamic to be healed, but will it
be? Sometimes, even when we've recalled the events that
triggered our phobia or other brought-through trauma,
we're still too 'human' to understand and forgive a past-
life crime or injustice. However, this person's bad feelings
of dread went away, so she must have accomplished what
her Soul Angel wanted her to.

It would of course be better if we all comprehended
that souls who've done us wrong in the past shouldn't be
blamed, because today they are only evolved from the

person they were then – they are not that person. This can be very difficult to do, though, and only very evolved souls are capable of this feat of forgiveness.

To travel in an opposite direction, some past-life recall can be quite amusing, even though all the while it explains and heals a person's attitudes. This particular woman was suffering from really bad lack of confidence and an inability to keep weight on. A very sweet person in this life, she was to change dramatically under hypnosis. The therapist told me that the change of character in her case was so extreme that it was verging on being funny. When such a strong change of character takes place, it adds greatly to the credibility of the regression.

My house is vast and no more than I deserve. I have a huge household of many servants and our house sits on the edge of a beautiful Scottish loch. I have a strong feeling that this man questioning me (the regressionist) *is far below my station, and I really feel he is being very impertinent. I tell him so, and demand that he show me more respect, even though I do feel compelled to answer his questions – he is, after all, only doing his job as a good servant should.*

I go to the market every week, taking some servants with me to carry my purchases. People seem to think me vain and bossy, but after all it is I who carries blue blood and not them! I don't have friends, but that doesn't bother me – I adore my own company.

These two things, low self-esteem and weight loss (or weight gain), often go together. It's that old chestnut of us not thinking ourselves worthy, and so we find it impossible to take care of our bodies. We tend to think if we overeat that we're 'treating' ourselves by allowing special foods like chocolate or anything rich. In fact we're punishing ourselves for some perceived past-life sin, just as someone who starves themselves is doing. In the example above, the woman in question obviously felt bad about her attitude to others in the past, and so she was overcompensating in this life by being too nice, and by not looking after herself. This all stopped once she understood her reasons for being that way. She continues to treat people politely and considerately, but doesn't overdo it!

This next session involved a very hard-nosed sceptic. It's interesting that past-life regression is the one area of the so-called 'paranormal' (although of course it's anything but) that people who claim not to believe in anything 'alternative' are actually willing to have a go at. They of course think they're doing it to discredit the practice, but of course I know they're doing it because, somehow or other, their Soul Angel has given them a successful nudge.

'I've never believed in angels or psychics or past lives or any of that flaky stuff. I'm a journalist and have always stayed objective and shied away from anything vaguely supernatural. But I have to admit I was driven to seek help from this unlikely quarter due to a problem I couldn't get rid of. I wanted to be an actor. Rather than writing the words, I wanted to be acting them out. I was passionate and determined and yet, every time I went for an audition, I flopped. My knees would quake and I'd not be able to utter a word. I'd go bright red and end up running off the stage in a panic and very scared. I didn't tell anyone how I felt because I was so embarrassed, but of course word got around and I felt everyone was laughing at me. I gave up for a while. But it wouldn't let me be. I'd have dreams of being an actor. The weirdest thing was that I never, ever got nervous before the audition. It was just when I walked on stage and saw the few seats that were filled with producers and directors. They were all looking at me, and that was it, I was finished.

'I'm not a shy person. I'll talk to anyone, interview anyone, so I didn't understand it at all. I went for all kinds of classes in self-confidence, etc., but I knew that wasn't the problem and I was right – they didn't make the slightest difference, just money and time down the drain. It was suggested that I go for hypnosis to cure the problem. I did, and it worked a little – enough for me to want to try again. It was on my second visit that something really odd happened. The hypnotherapist took me back through my life, searching for the cause of my problem, back and back, until suddenly, just like that, I found myself somewhere else – some*when* else. I was a scruffy young man, aged about 17, I think. I was wearing a rough leather jerkin and some sort of hessian-like trousers. I had no shoes on. I was being roughly manhandled along a cobbled road. The hypnotherapist asked me what year it was and I said with no hesitation, "1794." My brain was turning cartwheels by now, but I stuck with it.

'The men dragging me were wearing some sort of military uniform, and by their rough words and hands I figured I'd done something to upset the army. Next thing I knew, I was forced to the ground in front of a wooden device, and my head and wrists were soon clamped and locked into holes. A crowd of onlookers stood around shouting gleefully, and I felt incredible humiliation as they jeered at me. Then it really started. They began throwing stuff at me, nasty smelly rotten vegetables and any old rubbish they could lay their hands on. One man rushed out of a nearby house and threw the contents of a chamber pot in my face. It was filled with urine and faeces. I was hit and slapped, and all the time I felt trapped and helpless. They called me names, and what they said made me writhe with shame as well as pain. Finally I'd had enough and I asked the hypnotherapist to bring me out, which he did.

'Now I understood why standing on a stage with people watching me and shouting directions at me made me feel so afraid and so humiliated. It all made sense, but was it real? I can't say for sure, but from that day forth I have been cast in three plays – only small parts, but I never thought in my wildest dreams that I'd ever get that far.

'Do I believe in "flaky" past lives? I'm not sure, and if you asked me in person I'd probably say no, but if I'm honest, here where I'm not going to give you my name, I'd have to say … probably.'

Of course, I have no doubt this was all true. His Soul Angel definitely wanted him out of journalism. I suspect that very soon now he'll find himself led into a whole new type of life. Whether he believes in past lives or Soul Angels doesn't really matter, does it?

This next story illustrates how something you did in a past life can upset things for you in this one. Sometimes there's unfinished business in the past and our Soul Angel will nudge us to complete it. This is one of the things we'll have discussed in our conversations between lives.

'In this lifetime I fell in love with Samantha while she was living with another man, Greg. I couldn't let it go because the love was too strong, even though perhaps I felt I should have done. Samantha was weak, though, and couldn't tell Greg about us. Then she got pregnant. It wasn't his, I trusted her on that because she hadn't had sex with him for years by then – their partnership had become purely platonic. I went for past-life regression really to see what I could find out that might make Samantha leave with me before it was too late and the baby showed. I just couldn't understand what Greg's hold on her was. I've always believed in past lives.

'I discovered that Samantha and I had lived in Ireland during the 1600s. In that life I was the woman and Samantha was the man, Francis. Francis's father was Greg in this life. He tried to split us up, and so we decided to kill him. Together we drowned him while he was out in a boat. We knew we wouldn't be harassed any more with Francis's father gone. Francis died of consumption, and I died in a freak accident in a storm, years later.

'Now that Samantha knows why she feels compelled to stay with Greg, just from the guilt of that life, even though she loves me, I think we'll be able to find a way forward. She knows now that it's wrong to keep up the pretence of love just out of guilt.'

This guilt would have been sent by both their Soul Angels when they seemed in danger of going off track – i.e. not being together as they had contracted to be. Now that they know the truth they can also release Greg so that he too can find real happiness. Without the regression this would have ended with four lives ruined, including that of the baby.

Illness, especially of the kind that seems difficult if not impossible for the medical profession to get to grips with, such as ME, can often turn out to be a nudge.

A woman called Nadine was diagnosed with ME, the 20th-century environmental disease, which made her painfully reactive to almost everything in life.

> 'I could barely walk, let alone think or imagine going out. My body's immune system had collapsed. I was living in hell. A meal would knock me out for hours; walking down a street caused my glands to enlarge in pain and my breathing to become asthmatic; crowds terrified me, travel the same. In dark moments, and there were many, filled with confusion, pushed down and grovelling on my hands and knees, I would sob over and over again "Mother, Father, Sister, Brother! Where are you?" Who is this imaginary family? What is happening to me? Why am I so terrified of trains, of crowds, of people?

'A three-month hospitalization only confirmed my disabilities.'

Nadine's Regression

I'm a child running on a train platform. Crowds of people are being herded into boxcars. Chaos and panic permeate the air, which is pierced with sirens. The skyline, cold grey, is sheared with black smoke. I'm a five-year-old boy who has lost his mummy. I run backwards and forwards, jostled among the mass of bewildered people. I spot my mother's black hat with the peacock feathers. As I run towards her along the frostbitten platform, uniformed soldiers emerge out of the crowd. Menacingly they shout orders. I must get to my mother and her warm, protective body. Suddenly, I reel as searing cold steel glances across my temple. I feel sick and strange. A man scoops me up as he runs along the platform. All goes black. I'm on a train, swaying, jostling, dizziness, coldness, blackness. Then no clothes! Where are my clothes? Where is my mummy?

The stone floor is so cold. I'm shoved along, crowded together with others through a concrete underpass into a room – a shower room. The door seals shut. The water taps with the warm water we've been promised don't work; that yellow mist coming down must be steam but everything is still cold. I cough! I choke!

Nadine explains what happened afterwards:

'During that past-life session, in October 1991, every single symptom I'd become familiar with all through my life was triggered. The feeling of dying was such a part of me, I had known no other way of being! From that day my symptoms dropped away. What is interesting is that I'd taken the lid off a scenario I'd feared but had never allowed myself to see. For almost a year, I was in an amazing recovery mode: eating what I wanted, going on tube trains, busy crowds not the least concern, no longer obsessed with loneliness, winter not even a bother. The memory had been brought to light and released. The miracle I had hoped for had come. Then recently my allergies began to re-emerge. I did another therapy session in which I realized that I was reflecting patterns from my mother. And my daughter was replicating the same patterns. I also came to the awareness that a part of me was reacting to the spectre of the Nazis rising again like damned spirits out of their Second World War bunkers. Once I recognized that the images of the neo-Nazis returning to Germany were re-stimulating my patterns, I could release them. My whole life is now changed. My symptoms dissolved back into their hell-place. I have balanced my relationships, and feel I am beginning a new and healthy life.'

CHAPTER 8

Soul Angels and Animals

Do animals have Soul Angels? Well yes, of course, because our Soul Angels are with us all the way through every single existence we've ever had, and our souls travel through every life-form group on the planet. Our Soul Angels guide us from our original creation, when we first become separated from their whole and are laid down as sparks in the ground. Our progress, with our Soul Angels alongside, takes us through the times of soul fragmentation – that is to say, when our souls are split into multiple parts in order to be housed in the physical bodies of one of the lower life forms, such as 2,000 individual insects. Gradually, as each soul comes back to spirit, slightly developed by its experiences, its divisions become smaller and smaller in number, until we might become divided into two cows, or two cats for instance. At this point there is potential for the soul to become whole on the death of one of the pair. This will mean that the soul is ready to be housed in a human body.

Becoming a human is not, however, the spiritual equivalent of the Holy Grail. In many ways animals are more spiritually evolved than we are. It is our life within them that prepares us to be able to cope with being human and retaining, or regaining, our spirituality whilst being bombarded with all the emotional upheavals and all the materialistic priorities that we'd otherwise be overwhelmed by. Without having experienced the balanced energy of animals, we would never be able to cope with being human and remaining spiritual at the same time.

Animals don't live the way we do, always wanting more in the future. They live in the present and are much more firmly united with their instinctual souls than we are. Hence they don't lose their ability to intuit, for instance, the presence of water in an apparently arid place, or which foods they should eat to resolve a health issue naturally or maintain a healthy weight. You never see a fat wild animal – the only fat animals are those pets we have fed and taught to be greedy.

If you consider that true spirituality means a united and balanced mind, body and spirit, you can see why I say that in some ways animals are more spiritually evolved than we are.

So, yes, animals have Soul Angels. However, these angels play a much less intrusive part in their wards' lives than they do when their wards are living human lives, because animals are naturally more spiritual and in tune with the angels, and so don't need the same kind of attention.

Some people doubt that animals have a soul at all, but animals play a much more important guiding role in our lives than they're given credit for. If animals didn't have souls they wouldn't be capable of this. In many ways they are our teachers. Have you ever seen a white dog treat a brown one differently because it's a different colour, or because it was fat or what we'd consider 'ugly'? Did you ever see an animal treat a human differently because they were famous? Celebrity means absolutely nothing to animals, because they see us as all the same. We should follow their example and accept that whatever the skin colour, or perceived fame or class, we are all the same beneath our outer envelope.

By allowing themselves to be reincarnated into animal bodies that will be owned by a human, pets also give us the opportunity to learn compassion and empathy with others. Children who grow up learning these gifts from their pets, instead of just owning them as playthings, will grow up into much better adults. Not only that, but certain advanced animal communicators, such as Madeleine Walker, have told me that they've discovered that apparent behavioural problems in pets are actually often the animal's way of flagging up problems in their owners that originated in past lives they spent with each other. This implies that we have a soul group not only of humans who have walked alongside us through multiple lives, but of animals who have lived many lives with us.

Our Soul Angels work in tandem with the Soul Angels of our pets. Soul Angels in animals' bodies generate behaviour in our pets that flags up our problems, and so the animals further facilitate our spiritual growth, and give our Soul Angels another string to their bow when it comes to nudging us back to full spiritual awareness.

I'd like to give you an example of how this works.

Janice of Cheltenham was afraid of dogs all her life, so much so that it really affected her in her everyday life. She was nervous walking down any street lest a dog should be in a garden she was passing and might startle her, so she'd walk on the kerbstones near the road edge. No matter how friendly a dog might appear, she couldn't bear to be within a few feet of it. So her friends and family were naturally astounded when at the age of 30 she had a sudden and irresistible impulse to buy a German shepherd puppy. They all warned her that the breed could be naturally aggressive and needed a really strong and confident 'leader', but she was powerless to resist buying the puppy.

Janice found Jack after an email acquaintance 'coincidentally' sent her a bulk email about puppies needing homes. Janice said one look in the puppy's eyes and she was helpless, knowing that she was connected to this dog. Jack became her constant companion. No one was really surprised when Jack started to show aggressive tendencies towards other dogs, even at the young age of seven months, because it was obvious to them that Jack was absorbing Janice's fear and acting accordingly. He was worse when he seemed to be trying to protect Janice from other dogs, and considerably better if someone else walked him, which only seemed to confirm her friends' beliefs. Janice, however, thought otherwise, and this was given credence when many experienced dog trainers tried, and failed, to calm Jack down. As soon as a dog approached his mistress, Jack acted as if he wanted to kill it. Eventually, not wanting to part with her pet soul mate and desperate to stop his dangerous behaviour, Janice went to a pet regressionist. This is what Jack told her.

'Jack lived another life as a Siberian husky, called Akira, and Janice lived in this life too. Her name was Anatoli, a man. He was a worker on the Trans-Siberian railway in 1842. Anatoli lived a lonely life in a shack with just his dog Akira for company. Anatoli had no family and just worked to survive. Akira would sometimes hunt small animals and bring the kill back to share with his master, otherwise they would both have starved. One day when the two of them were making their way into a nearby town they were set upon by a pack of Siberian wild dogs. It was a horrifying attack. Akira killed many of the pack before he was taken down by weight of numbers, and both he and his owner were brutally torn apart.'

This explained at once both Jack's behaviour and Janice's fear. It also explained why, after fearing all dogs, when confronted with Jack she had felt compelled to take him home and make him her protector. Jack told the regressionist that he was overprotective now, both to flag up the cause of Janice's fear and also because he felt guilty at not having been able to save his owner in that past Siberian life. This guilt was healed for him, and since the regression Jack's 'fighting talk' with other dogs has disappeared. He even has a local 'friend' that he plays with. Janice, now that she knows where her fear comes from, and that the average domestic dog doesn't roam in wild packs seeking prey, can cope with and control her fear. She's even talking about visiting a zoo to get up close to some wolves.

Another way that our pets can show us that they were with us in past lives is when their Soul Angel helps them to change their appearance briefly into the way they once looked in another life shared together, so giving us a nudge towards remembering that particular past life. This is another example of how a person's Soul Angel and a pet's Soul Angel can cooperate to help us.

Jan of Horsham tells me:

> 'One night several years ago I was sitting in the lounge, surrounded by my crystals, which I was sorting out, with my Egyptian Mau cat Simba sitting in front of me, watching. I looked up from what I was doing and Simba and I looked at each other. As our eyes met, something unbelievable happened. I saw Simba's face and body change slowly into a completely different cat. His whole being changed and he was much, much, thinner in shape, along with having a completely differently coloured coat! I knew straight away he was my cat from a past life. Then his features turned back to Simba, and he just smiled at me! It was an amazing moment, one I'll never forget.'

Michael, a radio presenter in Adelaide, had this experience of three Soul Angels cooperating. They were his, his dying mother's, and his beloved cat's:

'A certain day in 2005 was particularly fateful for me. After a few months of worsening dementia along with lung fibrosis, my mother had to be taken to hospital for care as it could no longer be done at home. After some resistance, this was achieved and the afternoon and evening were spent in the hospital with various checks and diagnoses being made. At one point, I had to physically restrain her from removing the tubes that were in her body, while she stated calmly, "What do you have to do to die around here?" This was a symptom of the dementia; not her normal outlook. Eventually, a doctor suggested I go home as there was nothing else I could do there.

'So I got the bus home and was walking the few minutes from the stop to my place when I saw Isis, one of my two cats, lying on the footpath, not moving. He (yes, he) had obviously been hit by a car, probably in the previous day or two. He liked to wander, so not seeing him for that long had not been thought unusual. There didn't seem to be any major physical damage but he had certainly left us by that stage. A dramatic and horrible day? Yes, you could say that.

'One of my psychic friends picked up that there was an undiagnosed small tumour in Isis's head that would have got worse, and that since cats are one of the few creatures who can choose their time of leaving, he chose to spare me the upset, tears and expense of seeing that happen and trying to get it treated. Given his caring disposition, that doesn't surprise me. There may have been an added dimension to that as well because, not long afterwards, my mother started seeing a cat in her visions (many of which were odd by the very nature of the dementia, but the experiences of dementia patients must have the spiritual basis everything else does, by my estimation). This cat was apparently great fun and loved to dance to entertain people. It wasn't the large long-hair grey tabby that Isis was, so maybe it was another animal, or another incarnation of him. I just find the timing of this second cat's appearance interesting in context.

'It was also interesting to have the experience of walking through a couple of different shopping centres in the weeks afterwards, to twice have the in-store music play the song "Mr Bojangles". This has the line, "The dog up and died / After 20 years he still grieves," which made itself very clear to me – even more so when it happened the second time! I literally got the feeling that the message was exactly what I thought it was – a musical embodiment of my own grieving. Another psychic friend also suggested that it might also be Isis's message to me about how he feels, too. However, that was made even more apparent when, not long after his passing, I just sent a general thought to him saying, "You'd better be waiting for me when it's my turn to go." As clearly as I've ever heard anything, I got the immediate reply, "I promise."'

Our pets are often helped by their Soul Angels to interact with us in other ways, just to bring us comfort after they've died, such is the love they feel for their very special owners, owners they have been with in other lives. Sometimes they pop back, if only very briefly, in another animal's body.

Other pets are so special to us, and we to them, that they back come to be with us after they've died.

Wendy of Boston, Lincolnshire, told me her story of her kitten, Scampi:

'When Scampi was 12 days old, his Persian mother, Jessica, disappeared and she was never found. Scampi and his four sibling kittens were left alone and hungry in a basket on the top shelf of a remote shed on our farm. Only the kittens' pitiful mewing alerted me to the problem when just by luck I was passing the shed one day. All five kittens had crawled out of the basket, searching for food, and fallen over six feet down onto a cold concrete floor.

'One had already died, and the other four were cold and hungry, so I quickly stuffed them beneath my sweater, against my skin to keep them warm. Then I drove the one-and-a-half miles home. There I filled a hot-water bottle and wrapped them up with it to get them warm, and prepared a jar of powdered cat milk, feeding each one with a small syringe.

'I continued to do this for the next three weeks, getting up every two hours to feed them. I'd put them in an empty fish tank, and would leave the light on to keep them warm, and I kept the hot-water bottle underneath them at all times. I had to wipe their bottoms and keep them clean, even bathing them on occasion to keep them smelling nice. And, so that I never woke the rest of the household by setting an alarm and getting up so frequently, I'd drink a huge glass of water at the end of each kitten feed so that before the two hours were up I'd be bursting for the loo, and so I'd know it was time to get up and feed the kittens.

'Even the night I had to take my son to the airport, I took the kittens with me so that they never missed a feed, and eventually they grew to be able to eat solid food and use a litter tray. There was Chooch-Chee, a long-haired tabby female, Chip, a silver tabby male, Jessica, also a silver tabby, and Scampi, a long-haired blue-grey male and the rascal of the bunch. I still gave them a bottle of milk each day, but Scampi was never prepared to wait his turn. He'd run up my leg, right up to my shoulder, snuggle beneath my chin and down to my lap, and shove aside whomsoever I was feeding at the time.

'As they grew I knew I could never part with Scampi, but one night he became ill. I had no idea what had happened to him, and then discovered my young son had been playing with him and had dropped him. I was frantic. Scampi appeared lifeless. I'd just been attuned for reiki first degree, and I called upon the help of the angels, and before my very eyes I saw Scampi bathed in emerald light. Seconds later he started to purr. Another minute and he was up and running again, as if nothing untoward had ever happened. I was delighted!

'I sold his brother and sisters, and Scampi stayed with us. He became such a handsome cat. Beautiful, long, flowing dark grey-blue fur and amber eyes; he was stunning! We taught him, or he taught himself, to play fetch, chasing balls of screwed-up paper and bringing them back in his mouth and dropping them at our feet. He would play this game till he was puffed out. He followed us everywhere, got on well with our old cat Smokey (now 17) and, whenever we were gardening, there he'd be watching, taking an interest, and we'd tell him what we were doing and why.

'He was almost a year old when tragedy struck. He'd been watching my husband repair our son's bicycle tyre, and so the pair of them and Scampi were on the roadside when a car came speeding towards them. My husband thought Scampi was in the garden when the car thundered past, but he was still on the roadside and he'd decided at that moment to run across the road to the garden. The car hit him head-on. Scampi somersaulted three times, six feet in the air. My husband knew he had to be dead before he hit the ground. He shouted for me and I came running, scooping Scampi off the road, and I laid him on the lawn in the garden. I could see his soul was long gone, only his body twitched. I held him and spoke to him till he was still, then I sat a while talking to his soul, because I was sure it was nearby. I told his soul to look for the light and go towards it. We buried Scampi in the garden that day, 1 August 2007, and cried our tears.

'That night I stood outside in the dark and I called him, as I used to do. A cat ran from the grave up the drive and out onto the road. I knew it was him. That night I felt him walking along the bed on top of me, coming up to my face, and I reached out a hand to stroke him, knowing I wouldn't really be able to. I felt him settle at my feet to sleep, though he and Smokey had never slept in the house, having their own shed in the garden to sleep in where I'd lock them in at night.

'On 1 November, All Saints Day, I went to get Smokey

up for her breakfast. In the box in the shed where she lay curled, I saw Scampi lying there beside her. I couldn't believe my eyes. I turned away and looked back and he was still there. I spoke his name and told him I loved him, and when I looked away and then back again he had gone.

'Scampi had so short a life, yet he enriched ours with his. His memory lives on, and though he is missed, we know he is still with us, unseen, but on one day a year I know I'll see him again, so, I look forward to 1 November so much.'

There is even more to this idea of being connected to our pets. I know that we keep the biggest part of our soul in spirit, sending only a fragment of it to the Earth plane in order to energize our physical envelope or body. But we are also able to send a soul fragment into another body which will live alongside us and help and strengthen us, and this body is normally that of a pet. So, when you have one of those very special animal companions whom you feel so close to it's almost like they are a part of you, then in fact they probably *are* a part of you. In other words, you and your special pet are part of the same soul and are not separate. Because there are then two parts of your soul on the Earth plane at one time, you support one another.

When this pet dies, of course it's a terrible wrench, because you have lost a part of your support system, but it may help you to know that the fragment of your soul that was in the pet will go straight back to the whole, and so in fact you will never really be parted. It also means that this pet can easily return to you in another body, if your soul requires it.

CHAPTER 9

Past Lives and Suicide

As a child and young adult, I was taught that suicide was a sin. Even today people are told, if a loved one has killed themselves, they'll be subject to eternal damnation. What a terrible and totally wrong thing to teach people! What a dreadful thing to say to someone who's trying to cope with the sudden and tragic loss of a loved one. When someone close to you kills themselves, there are many more emotional traumas to deal with than if the person has died naturally or in an accident. This is because you feel they've deliberately abandoned you, perhaps because of something you did wrong or something you did not do, and especially if they were a parent, a child, or a partner, and the last thing you want to be told is that they are now lost to you for ever, consigned to some dark corner of hell. It isn't true.

How can I state this so categorically? Because I know that in a past life I killed myself, and yet here I am, back with another chance.

I'm not condoning suicide. Far from it. People contemplating such a thing should be aware that they will still come back to earth, and if they kill themselves because they can't handle their problems, then they won't escape but, like me, will have to face those same problems, or something very similar, again. For if we kill ourselves, then we won't fulfil what we came here to do, and so we'll agree to come back and try again. In one of my past lives I threw myself from a rooftop because I feared my lover was dead, and thought I could see him below me. I couldn't face life without him, so I opted out. I wasn't sent to hell, though. I wasn't berated or condemned as a sinner. I was, after an interval, sent back to get it right. So, in this lifetime my husband Tony, whom I really do love more than life, was struck down with a life-threatening illness, and much though I felt like running away, or hiding from the problem, this time I stood by my soul mate and tried to be strong for his sake. I accepted the challenges, though it filled me with horror, and somehow I coped. He's now well again.

There are a frightening number of young people today committing suicide, and I believe that a lot of this is preventable. In total more people per year kill themselves than are killed in wars – a million a year, in fact. The numbers have increased by 50 per cent in the last 60 years. These figures are terrible. One of the peak ages for suicide, especially in men, is just 20.

Some people who commit suicide are addicted – to food, to drugs, to drink, to gambling or to sex, or it can manifest as many other different obsessions. It can be OCD (obsessive compulsive disorder) with something like cleaning or personal hygiene or little rituals. There's usually a past-life reason for their obsession, and it's often that they were either addicted in the past and have come back to try and resist the temptation in this life, and failed, or that the object of their obsession reminds them of a happy past life and they 'overdose' on it in an attempt to recreate that happiness, which in fact is not possible in this life. However, these can all be overcome with the help of a good past-life regressionist, because once an addiction is seen really clearly for what it is, the victim can shake it off.

Josie from New York was a very pretty young woman in her early twenties. She seemed to have everything going for her, except for one thing – she found it impossible to be faithful. She'd lost Steve, the man she claimed was the love of her life, because he'd found out that she was sleeping with other men behind his back. One of the odd things was that the men she slept with were always at least 20 years older than her. She preferred men aged about 45. She said she felt compelled to do this because it made her feel 'safe', which seemed like a bizarre reason, to say the least. Josie was on the verge of suicide and had actually made feeble attempts to end her own life twice by the time she tried past-life regression.

> I'm 16 years old and my name is Katrina. I work in a brothel just outside Las Vegas. I'm really happy here living in my trailer and being treated like a queen. Walter's my boss and he's the sweetest man to me. I was born in a trailer park and never had a family since I was three years old. I was fostered out to some really nasty people who abused me. When Walter took me in I had no friends and was about starving to death. Here I have friends, sisters and Walter to take care of me. I don't ever want to leave the ranch.

Katrina got her wish in that life, and died at the brothel after a fire. She'd been badly injured, and died a few weeks later with Walter at her side.

When Josie saw the reason for her sex addiction, she was amazed and also immediately changed. She could understand the reasons and knew that she wouldn't need to have sex with multiple older men in order to feel safe ever again. She could see she'd been living a fantasy and not her real life, which was with Steve.

The incredible aftermath to this story is that Josie persuaded Steve to be regressed, too, and he turned out to have been none other than her former boss, Walter. Once he saw the reality of how their life had been before, Steve was able to forgive Josie for her unfaithfulness, and they embarked afresh on their relationship.

Depression is of course the biggest cause of suicide, and young people have a lot to be depressed about: being sent to war, or starving to death (in Third World countries), or carrying the burden for raising and supporting a family. The biggest cause of depression in the young is often lack of self-belief and self-worth, and no sense of purpose. If only these young people could be shown the whole of their wondrous selves, and come to understand that what they see on the surface is just the tip of the iceberg of their being, they would surely feel they are here for a purpose. Past-life regression shows them all of this. Done correctly, it also takes them through their previous death and sometimes into their between-lives state. When this is done they can see that there is no purpose to suicide, but there certainly *is* a purpose to their life here.

Still, sometimes a soul just gets too weary to carry on, and in that case they go back to spirit and are allowed to rest. There is no hell, and we are living lives to learn, not to be punished. We are held and loved and guided, and if we make a mistake, then yes, of course we will eventually have to put that right, but suicides are not loved any less by the angels, or cared for any less than any other soul. Suicide is not a sin, it's a mistake, and the idea of God punishing someone for all eternity over a mistake is, frankly, in my eyes, blasphemy.

Here are some examples of people who made this 'mistake', and how they made up for it in their next life. We hear first from Patricia, from Coventry.

I'm a young girl, fresh, pretty and innocent. It's 1692, and I'm living on the streets of London. My ma died when I was small, and I never knew my father. I was handed over to some nuns and they took care of me and brought me up right, but I didn't want to become one of them. They taught me well, and I'm grateful to them, but I need to make my own way. It was dull in the abbey and I longed for excitement and a wild life. I've been on my own for two years and now I'm wondering if I made the right choice. The streets are mean and, after dark, men are always following me. I'm always cold, sometimes even in summer, and always hungry. One day I meet another girl, and she tells me there's a way I can make money, more than I ever dreamed of. I let myself be persuaded and I follow her to a house. Once there I realize I've been tricked, but it's too late. I get locked in a room.

Days pass and they send men to me. These men have paid to lay with me, and if I resist I'm beaten. I'm so ashamed. I think of the sisters, especially Sister Agnes, as the men use me, and my body burns with embarrassment. The sisters would be so ashamed of me. One night after a few weeks, I get the chance to escape when a window's left open. Finally, faced with a way out, I can't make myself take it. I'm too ashamed to go back to Sister Agnes. I'm too afraid to go back on the streets, for surely I'll find myself back here, or in another just-as-foul place before long. So, I balance a chair on the bed, and climb up to pass the cord that serves for my belt over the bare rafter above. I pass the loop around my own neck and I jump, with barely a thought in my head as I die.

Patricia realized that Sister Agnes, whom she kept thinking of the most, was her mother in her current life. In this life Patricia had become pregnant aged 14, and been faced with another terrible dilemma. She was incredibly ashamed to tell her mother she was pregnant, as this was back in the 1950s, when girls who got pregnant were very badly treated, and carried the entire stigma themselves, with no blame placed on the boy. But this time Patricia had not opted out of life. She'd told her mother she was expecting, and was forgiven and cherished. Finally, at age 60, having just then had the regression, Patricia realized that as Sister Agnes, the woman who was her mother this time would have forgiven her and taken care of her back then as well. Her mother was still alive when the regression took place, aged 80, and Patricia was able to repay her by promising to care for her for the rest of her life.

Here is Andrew's story, which demonstrates two things. It's another case of someone who killed themselves in a past life and yet still found that the causes came back to haunt him in this one. It's also a useful demonstration of how finding out something bad you did in a past life doesn't mean you have to continue to feel guilty or be unhappy in this life.

Andrew was a successful 28-year-old stockbroker working in the posh southern California city of Newport Beach when he sought out hypnotherapy for a lifelong struggle with depression. He reported having gone through years of traditional mental-health counselling, which had helped him to understand that his thoughts were responsible for his feelings. And yet, even armed with this knowledge, he felt that something was still there, blocking him from being a happy person. By the time he came in for a session he was desperate for some relief. 'I have all the right reasons to be happy,' he said. 'I live in a beautiful home by the ocean. I'm financially successful but I don't *feel* happy when I wake up in the morning. In fact, I have had a deep sense of guilt and sadness that has been with me for as long as I can remember.'

Andrew's Regression

First of all I found myself back in my current childhood, hearing again my mother's strident voice criticizing me and verbally abusing me for making mistakes. ('I was a sensitive child and her constant berating made me grow up into a perfectionist in an attempt to avoid further criticism. In some ways this paid off, as it made me excel in my work, but the burden of always trying to be perfect made it impossible for me to ever be truly content, because which one of us is really perfect all the time? Using guided imagery, my therapist helped me to speak my truth to my mother, which helped me to release the old painful feelings I had about those childhood memories. When I came out I felt better, but I still had feelings of guilt and some sadness, so she asked me to follow the sadness and guilt back in time, "How far back can you go and still have the awareness of the sadness and guilt being there?" she asked me. I responded, "Even beyond birth." She suggested we try past-life regression.')

It's the time of the Second World War. I'm a young man living in a small village in Germany. I've been taken in by the speeches of Adolf Hitler. When the German troops come to my village, I admire them and desire their respect.

Later

I've done something terrible. I've reported some Jews who were hiding with our neighbours. The Jews have been shot, and our friends hanged in the town square, to warn others who might 'betray' Germany. I thought I was doing the right thing, but when I see them killed I know that I've been mistaken. I've made a terrible mistake! My mother never forgives me and the townspeople shun me. My guilt and shame are immense. I go into the woods and die alone.

'At this point in the session, I began to cry. I realized that I have the same mother in this life as I did in Germany. It's why she has been so hard and critical of me in this life. My therapist asks me to go to the time right after I died in the woods, when my soul left my body. She asks me what I have learned. "I don't have the right to be happy after what I've done." I responded. "I've learned how precious life is. I've learned the value of loyalty and withholding judgement on others."

'She tells me, "If wisdom erases karma, can you give yourself permission to release the guilt and sadness that you carried forth from that life?"'

A year later, Andrew contacted his therapist to let her know that he had made peace with his mother and with himself. He had stopped working so hard, had found a girlfriend and had started volunteering at a charity in his community. 'Life is good,' he told her.

CHAPTER 10

Children and Past Lives

It never fails to amaze me the number of children there are who can remember snippets of their past lives. Quite often, of course, their mentions of another time or person are pooh-poohed as imaginary, but on some occasions the proof is very convincing.

XENOGLOSSY

Jamie, from Ohio, was a jolly little two-year-old boy, and a joy to his parents, apart from one worrying thing. He was very slow to start talking, or so his parents thought. He made sounds and they soon noticed that he had his own little vocabulary of sorts, because certain sounds were repeated consistently for the same objects. If he wanted a drink he'd say what sounded like 'iki'. For Mommy he'd say 'seziz', and for Daddy he'd say 'baba'. The last one had them totally confused, as they thought he was repeating what they called his three-month-old brother. It wasn't until a friend called round that the mystery was solved: Jamie was speaking Turkish. The family had never even been to Turkey. By the time Jamie was four this had pretty much faded and he'd reverted to English.

This was a classic example of what's called *xenoglossy*, which means someone speaking in a language they could not know naturally nor have learned. Dr Ian Stevenson has done a huge amount of research into this subject. Most children, as with Jamie and most of us who have any kind of spiritual connection, lose the ability by around the age of seven. However, sometimes it can come back.

Czech speedway rider Matej Kus from Pilsen had a terrible accident in 2007, aged 18 years. When he came round after a spell of unconsciousness, for a short time he was able to speak perfect English, even though he had never known the language during his lifetime. After a few hours the ability vanished again, most likely back into his past life.

OTHER PARENTS
Imagine you're playing with your daughter, just like any other day. She's maybe aged around four or five years old.

Suddenly she says to you, 'Before you were my mummy, I had another mummy.' At first you think you've misheard, but she repeats it with conviction, as if you're being silly not to understand. These words can cause shock, outrage and disbelief. You question your child, for what can she possibly mean by saying, 'another mummy'?

'My other mummy – you know, before I was in your tummy, I lived with my other mummy.' By now it's quite clear what she means, and you know she's obviously talking about another lifetime. This realization can cause terrible pain to a parent.

An amazing number of parents have actually had this conversation with their child and been heartbroken by it. After all, this is *your* child, the one you created and the one who is totally unique to you. This is the child who grew inside her mother, and came into the world in a rush of love, to spend her life with your family. You have a special, unbreakable bond with her. How can you come to terms with the thought that she was actually another person in a previous life, possibly one who grew into adulthood without you, calling someone else 'Mummy' or 'Daddy'?

Other parents have told me that they're very upset by these revelations, because if their child has lived before, then he or she will surely live again and they're filled with horror at the thought that, not only will they have to say goodbye to their child at some point, they will also have to face the fact that their child may well go on to be *someone else*, and someone else's child. Their child will be born to other parents and who knows how they'll be treated by them? It's all too much for them to grasp.

This very natural reaction must be of great frustration to the child's Soul Angel, who up to that point has probably been congratulating itself on having scored an 'early goal', in that their ward still has his or her spiritual connection intact.

There is a way parents can deal with this. When the child says these things, remember it's not to hurt you. To the child, he or she is just stating a fact. He or she was with another mummy, but now (and most importantly), the child is with *you*. This is your child in all his or her specialness, and that will always be the case. The past 'other parents' weren't really the parents of *your* child – they were the parents of the spirit your child has evolved from. And in the future, other parents won't be the parents of your unique child, either, but will be the parents of the child who has evolved from yours.

Sue-Ann, in Oklahoma, aged four years, was heard talking to an 'invisible' person in the room, and when asked by her mother, Grace, whom she was talking to, announced quite calmly and without inflection, 'My other mom.' Grace assumed at first that Sue-Ann was just playing, perhaps talking about her doll's imaginary family, but then the child went on to say, 'She was my mom when there were four of us kids, before I was borned here. My mom and dad both had long grey hair, and dad had a big beard but no moustache, no moustaches allowed! Our house was all made of wood and we had a horse called Daisy, and a cart and no car.'

Now strongly suspecting that her daughter was talking about another life, and that it was about having been Amish, Grace asked her, 'What was your name, and the names of the other children?'

'My mom and dad were Zooks, and my name was Mary and my brothers were Samuel and Jacob. My little sister was Rebecca.'

The choice of names was spot on, and the best part about this tale was in the child's reference to moustaches not being allowed. How would a four-year-old know that Amish men are forbidden to wear moustaches (because of their association with the military)?

The very 'matter of factness' a child will use when talking about these things is what makes the words so compelling as regards past-life evidence. When a child is play-acting he or she will use a very typical sing-song voice, whereas when talking about actual memories there is none of that at all. The difference is very easy to spot.

PRODIGY

The most famous example of a child being born with a talent far exceeding their years is that of Mozart. At the age of four, he had already written a piano concerto. No child, however naturally talented, would normally be developed enough to achieve such a thing. This concerto was very technical, too, beyond the reach of most adults. At age seven Mozart composed a full-length opera. There is no mainstream explanation for this. It's just an impossibility, so the only logical answer is that he brought through skills from a previous life. So it is with most prodigies.

There are some other equally amazing child prodigies, such as:

- **Jean-Louis Cardiac, born in France in 1719. He knew the alphabet at three years old and by the time he was four he could speak and translate Latin fluently.**

- **In 1953 an eight-year-old girl called Giannella de Marco conducted the London Philharmonic Orchestra. The concert was the 123rd of her career, which had begun when she was only four years old.**

BIRTHMARKS

A lot of children get made fun of because they have birthmarks, but sometimes when the cause of them is discovered, the children take on the status of hero in the eyes of their peers.

A young boy aged ten came to me. He was terribly upset because he had a brown mark on his tummy which the other kids made fun of. He hated to go swimming or do anything that required him showing his tummy because of the other children. I discovered, by doing a physic past-life reading, just why he had the mark. This is what I told him:

'In 1830 you were a Comanche boy, who was sent on his first buffalo hunt when he was 13. His horse fell down and the boy was gored in the stomach by a male buffalo. Despite this, he still managed to spear the buffalo and kill it. He recovered from the wound and was esteemed because of the bravery he'd shown. He became initiated as a warrior, aged only 14, a year earlier than normal, and was eventually elected as a War Chief, an honour given only to the most respected men. He was called Buffalo Hump (*Po-cha-na-quar-hip*) and he was a very brave warrior.'

The boys at school don't laugh at him any more.

I've been provided with the answers to some of the questions that parents commonly ask when faced with possible past-life memories from their children.

WHY IS IT THAT CHILDREN RETAIN PAST LIVES SO MUCH MORE EASILY THAN ADULTS?

Children are much younger than their parents, and so they've been separated from their spirit for less time than their parents have. The memories are closer to the surface, and the surface isn't covered over by the cares of adulthood. This is the same reason that children can often see angels and spirits – they are more attuned to the spiritual world than their parents are.

WHY IS IT THAT CHILDREN'S PAST-LIFE MEMORIES FADE AT AROUND AGE SEVEN?

This seems to be the extent of time that children stay connected, no matter what. After that, apart from the odd exception, where their 'gift' is too strong to let go or they have parents who nurture their spirituality, the connection falters and gradually breaks.

WHAT SHOULD YOU DO WHEN YOUR CHILD REMEMBERS A PAST LIFE?

Try not to be shocked. Ask intelligent questions such as, 'What was your name? What year is it?' Do this without putting pressure on the child to try and get as much information as possible. Give gentle encouragement and take notes so that one day in the future, if your child needs it he or she can have access to those early memories. Listen for clues, such as mode of dress, types of buildings and vehicles – things that will help you pinpoint a time and place.

HOW DO I KNOW IF MY CHILD IS REALLY REMEMBERING A PAST LIFE OR JUST IMAGINING THINGS?

As I mentioned before, the matter-of-fact tone, quite unlike his or her usual 'playing' voice, is one clue.

Another is your child being consistent about his or her stories. With true memories there are no embellishments over time, and the details remain the same.

If your child undergoes a slight personality change during the telling, or speaks in a strange way with different phraseology from normal, that's another pointer that he or she is recalling a genuine past life.

If your child has unexplained talents, or is a 'natural' at doing something he or she has never been taught, this may have been brought through from a previous life.

If your child possesses particular knowledge about a subject, that's another convincing piece of evidence. For instance, one child I knew was able to dismantle, clean and reassemble a First World War rifle, at a trained soldier's pace, at age four.

Afterword

- **What will happen if I go for regression?**

- **What does it feel like?**

- **How can I find a good past-life regressionist?**

- **Can I be hypnotized?**

So, perhaps you've been getting nudges that have prompted you to think it's time you found out about your own past, or this book has convinced you, but perhaps you're a bit apprehensive? I hope to put your mind at rest on that score. What precisely happens when you're regressed? Should you worry about handing control of yourself over to someone else? Will you know what you're saying, or will you be unconscious and vulnerable, and have an idea planted in your head by the hypnotist or be made to act foolishly?

You don't need to worry about any of these things, so long as you choose an experienced, correctly trained therapist, which you will know precisely how to do by asking the questions listed below.

In the meantime, I'll answer other questions I'm frequently asked.

HYPNOTHERAPY

You won't be unconscious or helpless while hypnotized. You'll be aware of what you're saying. A therapist will hypnotize you, which means you'll be able to reach a state of total relaxation. In this state you'll be able to access your Akashic records, which are filed away in your subconscious. At first you may be unsure, but once you start talking the floodgates will open and your entire history will be at your disposal.

A good hypnotherapist won't plant any ideas or feed you with any information, and all the questions you are asked will be open-ended, and not lead you down any pathways. He or she will merely ask your subconscious questions and allow it to answer. The questions will be like 'Is anyone with you?' rather than 'Who is with you?' The first allows your subconscious to answer freely either way, while the second makes your subconscious accept that someone *is* there. Likewise, 'Do you have anything on your feet?' rather than, 'What are you wearing on your feet?'

FINDING A THERAPIST

Once you've decided that finding out about your past life, both to stop the nudges from your Soul Angel and to get your full memory back, is right for you, you need to know how to find the right therapist. One really good way is by personal recommendation from a friend. Another way is to read my monthly column in *Chat – It's Fate*, where you can see how the various therapists work, and select one of them.

It's advisable to ask your chosen therapist a few penetrating questions. Don't be shy or afraid to ask them. This could be the most important decision you've ever made, after all. If a therapist isn't willing to be asked questions, then walk away and find one who is.

THE QUESTIONS TO ASK

1. How much experience have you had of hypnotizing people, and treating them with past-life regression in particular?

2. What safeguards will you put in place, in case I'm very upset by what I see and I don't want to continue?

3. How will you tie up the regression and bring me back to my current life?

4. What will you do to heal my death in a past lifetime and take away my fear of dying?

5. What will you do to heal any traumas I remember and make sure they don't 'leak' into my current life?

6. What level of trance will I reach?

THE ANSWERS

These should be something along the lines of:

1. I have regressed many people into past lives, and have resolved their current life problems by enabling them to explore their past.

2. Before I take you deeply I will show you a safe place you can retreat to if things get too tough. From that place you'll be able to come out of the session at any time because you'll be able to tell me you've had enough.

3. I will take you right through your death in that life, so that the circle is completed and you can see the whole life in the right context.

4. I will bring you out to the light and let you look back and observe your body, so that you see that death is nothing to be feared. You'll know that it's natural to die and return, and that there is no end.

5. I will talk you through the traumas and discuss with you what you can learn from them. I will make sure that the trauma is released, healed and stays in the past, where it belongs.

6. I will make sure that you sink through the levels in stages, and that I will bring you back slowly through the levels, to make sure that you are fully detached from the past and can easily return.

LEVELS OF TRANCE

There are many levels of hypnotic trance, from seeing just a flickering snapshot of your past, like getting fuzzy TV reception, right through to actually re-experiencing the past as if it were happening right now.

LEVEL 1

This is not a very deep regression and you will only get glimpses of your past. As with most mediums' messages, the facts will be sketchy and you may well come out of the regression not quite sure if what you saw was real or just your imagination.

LEVEL 2

In this level the picture will be very clear; however, you will be viewing the events from a third-party perspective. Your emotional involvement will be only a little stronger than if you were watching an emotive film. It will all seem very familiar to you, but you won't be quite sure if this was something that happened to you or to someone else.

LEVEL 3

At this level you will be aware of taking part in the events that unroll in front of you, and you may experience very empathic senses, such as taste and smell. The tale will seem a little surreal, though, and you may not be complexly involved in it. There may be some confusion, and still you might feel as if the person taking part is not really you. This, as in the previous level, is because your body, mind and soul are not yet quite reunited, and so that aspect of you which lived the life you are viewing will still not feel quite like the real you.

LEVEL 4

At this point all the emotions are very real, and will stay with you for the rest of your conscious lives. You will be very absorbed, and all the senses will be fully experienced.

However, at this level you will still be peripherally aware of your current life and persona, and be aware that you are undergoing past-life memories. The character in the events will be easily thought of as 'I', but you will still answer the therapist's questions, using references to your current life, such as 'I was older than I am now.'

LEVEL 5

This is as deep as you can get. You will be totally immersed in the past life, and have no awareness of your current life. You will answer questions in the present tense, such as, 'I am walking down a narrow lane …' You will experience full detail and be aware of conversations, colours and moods. It is at this level that caution with choosing your therapist is vital.

Be aware that some people leap straight into Level 5, as I did. This was because my Soul Angel, who knows all, deemed that it was the right thing for me. It's a good idea, before you embark, to speak with your Soul Angel, as if it were another person. Just simply say out loud that you want to explore your own past, you feel ready to do so, and you are asking for guidance and protection through-out the procedure. You can trust your Soul Angel not to allow you to come to any harm.

CAN I BE HYPNOTIZED?

Some people worry that they won't be able to be hypnotized, so to reassure anyone who thinks that, I've included this account by a past-life regressionist, which describes how this concern might be alleviated and worked around, even when it looks insurmountable. The name of the client has been changed to protect her privacy.

'There are times, as a certified past-life regression counsellor, that I hear, "I can't be hypnotized, I've tried it before." While I'm careful not to set someone up for disappointment, I also usually require the potential participant to evaluate if they are creating this story about themselves, or if it is in fact reality. One way to determine this is to ponder if the person typically has a great need for control. I know it may seem a simple way to evaluate this, but if a person considers himself as someone who generally likes to have a great degree of control, he will ultimately tend to sabotage the ability to allow the great library of the subconscious mind to open and allow the memories and information to flow forth.

'So, I ask the person on a scale of one to ten how controlling he thinks he is. Almost 100 per cent of the time those who have had difficulty in the past with being hypnotized rate themselves a 7 to 10. Then I always ask,

"Are you willing to surrender control to have this experience?" If he says yes, and comes to the table willingly, he finds himself easily connecting without the previous perceived difficulty.

'One particular client was really desperate to try anything that would give her some clarity regarding a current relationship. Ann was married, but was feeling an increasing emotional connection with a man she worked with. She'd felt an instant connection to this man from the beginning, and found herself wandering into his office whenever she needed someone to talk to. He too was married. However, neither of them could deny the intensity of their connection. It became apparent that they were growing closer daily, and their conversations began to border on the inappropriate, considering their married status. Ann was not unhappy in her marriage; quite the opposite, in fact. However, the level of satisfaction gained both intellectually and emotionally from this co-worker was intoxicating, and as if drawn to him magnetically, Ann started finding herself thinking about him, not only in the office but also at home. Furthermore, she suddenly found herself wishing to be with him even when she was with her husband.

'Ann was in search of answers, and a need to understand her connection to this man, which from an outsider's perspective would be completely illogical, considering their significant age difference and contradicting life-styles. However, Ann was not able to stop the frequent thoughts and daydreams that seemed to haunt her both at work and at home. That is when she called me.

'On a scale of one to ten for control, Ann is a 10.5. Therefore, she was concerned, as was I, that this would present a challenge to the process of hypnosis. However, she also admitted that she had a feeling this connection to her co-worker was spiritual, and that therefore the problem wouldn't be solved with traditional counselling. We both agreed it would be worth the risk of attempting hypnosis, and that we would take this on in the light of experimentation, trusting that her spirit would guide the way to the understanding she sought.

'We began our conversation by clearing up any myths or preconceived notions regarding hypnosis and past lives. It immediately eased Ann's mind to learn she was not going somewhere she could not control or come back from on her own. I led her through a long and deep relax-ation. I took a much longer route to deepen her hypnotic state, since I could sense she was still apprehensive and tense during a good portion of the beginning relaxation. After almost 40 minutes of relaxation, I could physically see her body grow more limp and loose, and her eyes began to roll back and forth behind her eyelids, which was a great sign that she was entering a powerful place of rest and comfort. I continued the protocol, having her go back to happy scenes from this lifetime, and she was able to recall several with great accuracy and detail.

'After that, I led her into the doorway to one of her past lives. I began asking her questions. She remained silent for several minutes. I asked her again. Ann sighed and began shaking her head, "No." I could instantly tell she was resisting what was coming to her, so I asked her what was happening. She said, "I don't know." I usually preface sessions by telling clients they are not permitted to use that as an answer.

'After attempting several avenues of approaching the questions and answers, I continued to hear her say, "I don't know." Finally, she counted to five and opened her eyes, saying, "I don't think this is working for me." I honoured her fears completely and reassured her there was nothing wrong with her, it might just not be the best way to achieve the clarity and understanding she was hoping for.

'Being a psychic medium, I'm often guided in the best direction for each individual whom I sit with. Suddenly I was shown an image in my mind of Ann sitting at a computer typing a novel. I was gently urged by spirit to take Ann back into hypnosis quickly and to try yet another tactic, which I had never attempted before in the dozens of past-life regressions I'd facilitated.

'I encouraged Ann to try one last time, having been inspired by my spirit guides. She readily agreed, admitting that she was sceptical but still willing. The excitement began to build in the room, and we both felt a surge of hope that hadn't existed before. I immediately took Ann back into the deep hypnotic state she had achieved in the beginning of the session. Then I asked her to be herself, and to sit down at the computer to write a novel. It was going to be fiction or non-fiction, her choice. She chose non-fiction. Then I asked her what genre she wished to write, mystery, romance, or other. Ann chose romance. Then I asked her to begin writing the novel and to describe what was happening as she was both creating and writing the story.

'Ann was silent for some time. However, what happened next surprised us both. She began telling me the story she was writing as if it were playing out like a movie in her head. Ann was having difficulty keeping up with the typing on her computer as the story was coming to her faster and faster. I reassured her that I would do the typing for her and she could just tell me the story, not worrying about the typing any more.

'Ann said she was staying at a cottage with a man; she knew it was him … the co-worker in her current lifetime. Then she became emotional. She understood instantly that they were not allowed to be together, it was forbidden. Ann let go a tremendous sob, as if something in the pit of her stomach let loose and the waterfall of emotions that had been so pent-up were suddenly flowing freely, no longer being held back.

'Ann began describing the story with incredible clarity. It was just beautiful. Then she paused for a longer time and I asked her to fast-forward to something important that happened to them in that lifetime. She struggled, as if resisting what was to come, followed by more silence. Then she saw the man again. This time they were free; they had run away and could be together. However, it didn't end happily. She viewed this man being run over, crushed by a stampede of animals. It wasn't his fault. He'd been going to find food for them. The images came to Ann in such erratic and bold flashes that she could only grab onto them briefly. Ann saw her love's face just before he was trampled. As more of the scene unfolded, Ann understood he had fallen and hurt his leg. He could not get up, he could not run, he could hardly move because he had grown so weak. He died. Ann was crying and very upset.

'Just when they had finally been able to be together in that life, it had been snatched from them. Ann died a lonely death herself in that lifetime, and afterwards I led her out of the experience, with her having forgiven herself and anyone else who needed forgiving from that lifetime. The crying began to subside, and I brought her back to the present time to analyse and discuss this event.

'Ann could not believe how incredibly clear everything had been. Even though she'd had some doubts along the way that she might be making it up, she could not discredit the intensity of the emotional connection she felt to the entire process. It seemed to fill her with such incredible relief that she could now understand the roots of her connection with her co-worker and the nature of their relationship. Furthermore, she acknowledged her ability finally to find release. That helped her mind to let go.

'I did see Ann a short while after her regression. She was still married to the same man, and she thanked me for helping her find the truth about her connection to her co-worker.'

My final words really are about how you might feel now. I hope you've accepted that you have a Soul Angel and that it needs to bring nudges into your life, some of which may be unpleasant, all for your own spiritual good. I hope you feel an inkling of truth in the fact that you are part of that Soul Angel, so that these nudges are actually sent to you with your blessing. I hope you understand that it's likely that if you have these nudges, you've probably strayed off your rightful path and need steering back onto it. You should believe that if you can reconnect fully with your soul, your life will get very much better and the nudges will no longer be necessary. Despite all this, you may still be afraid to look into your past lives as a way of reconnecting. Please don't be afraid. I have never, in my 16 years of studying past-life regressions, heard of anyone being damaged by being regressed by an experienced therapist. If you have a fear of discovering something unpalatable about yourself, such as having been a bad person, do talk to your therapist about this. He or she will reassure you that even if that were to occur, he or she would also be able to heal any unnecessary guilt associated with that life (remember, you are no longer in that body), and also move you on to other lives, where you did good things, so that you feel a balance in your karma. Remember Andrew's past-life account in the chapter on suicide, for evidence that all things can be resolved, and all your negative actions from a past life need to be forgiven, especially by yourself. There can't be a much more unpleasant thing to discover about yourself in a past life than what Andrew recalled, and yet he was able to resolve it because he gained and accepted the wisdom it was meant to teach him, and he was able to move on in this life to happiness.

At worst, past-life regression is a quiet time of relaxation. At best it can change how you feel and how you live your life. It can remove fear and anxiety and give you a clear head so you can perceive your master plan. It can change how you see people you perhaps have problems with, and remove phobias by giving you the power that comes with knowledge. It can even sometimes resolve health issues. In this instance you do have to deal with all your bodies, including their physical form, because if your illness has caused damage to your body or its functions, it may still need medical treatment but you should be able to stop the condition recurring with your new-found knowledge of the cause. Past-life regression can help you re-evaluate your priorities and enable you to handle problems from a new perspective. Even if your life has seemed fine, imagine how much more potential there would be if you were walking in step with your angelic part. Reuniting in this way holds the best chance of true happiness.

This happiness you can attain is manifold:

1. Just by connecting more closely with your angel you'll be more open to a sense of joy, through knowing you can never be alone or feel unsupported again.

2. By understanding what your Soul Angel wants, and doing it, you'll remove all need for painful lessons and reminders and lead a happier, more relaxed life.

3. At the same time you'll be balancing and calming your energy, so that everything you ask your angels for becomes eminently more possible.

4. By reconnecting to your past lives you'll lose the amnesia of the soul that so many people in our world suffer from, and come to a new understanding of yourself.

5. Once your spirit is whole you have a very good chance of discovering your master plan, and with it you'll have also discovered the secret to real, enduring happiness that comes from within.

6. By gaining all this knowledge you'll also gain the power to be able to change your own life-script and create the reality you've always dreamed of.

Resources

http://www.lifebetweenlives.org.uk
http://www.pastliferegression.co.uk
http://www.iarrt.org/

Now that you've seen how your Soul Angel wants you to remember your whole being, and not just this lifetime's highlights, you've probably decided to take the plunge into your own history and get yourself regressed. This isn't as easy as it should be, because many hypnotherapists *still* don't advertise the fact that they do past-life regression. Of course, you can always ask if they do so, but to make things easier for you, I've compiled this worldwide comprehensive list of resources for finding a hypnotherapist who does past-life regression. All of these have given permission to be included in my list, although their inclusion does not necessarily mean they will be right for you, so please ask the questions I've compiled in the previous chapter to make sure you find the right therapist.

There are still a few places that don't seem to have any regressionists at all, and I find that very disappointing. Who knows, perhaps *you* are destined to train to do this work and fill in a gap. Anyway, in the meantime, hopefully you'll find one in your area. If not, email me and perhaps I can help: info@author.globalnet.co.uk.

There is only one pet/animal regressionist listed, in Somerset. However, should you need her services and live out of her area, she can also work remotely from a hair/feather/fur sample.

I'd like particularly to thank the following past-life therapists who very kindly contributed accounts of some of their regression stories and successes to this book:

Diana McManus

Graham Howes

Georgina Cannon

Mary Lee Labay

Madeleine Walker (animal regressions)

Rifa Hodgson

Delilah Rohman

Dr Tish Morgan

Judith Stone

Karen De Jager

Rebecca Shaw

Greg McHugh

Chandra Parkinson

Lorna Simmons

Jon RG Turner

ENGLAND

Berkshire

www.thepatienceclinic.com

Bristol

www.awakening2hypnosis.com

Buckinghamshire

www.hypnotherapyhighwycombe.co.uk

Cambridgeshire

www.changesinmind.com

Cornwall

www.pastliferegression.co.uk

Cumbria

www.soul-healing.org.uk

Devon

www.deja-view.org.uk

Dorset

www.pastliferegression.biz

Durham

www.pastliferegression.co.uk

East Midlands

www.nottinghamhypnotherapy.co.uk

Essex

www.pastlives-presenthealing.co.uk

www.teachingtherapies.com

www.peaceful-minds.com

Hampshire

www.innerpeacehypnosis.co.uk

Kent

www.holistichc.co.uk

Lincolnshire

www.vibranthealth.info

London

www.pastlifehealing.co.uk

www.the-apple-tree.co.uk

www.footprintsfromthepast.co.uk

www.ninepeachestherapies.com

Merseyside

www.merseyhypnosis.com

Norfolk

www.downhamhypnotherapy.co.uk

Northamptonshire

www.anaturaltoolbox.co.uk

North Yorkshire

www.hypno-therapists.co.uk

Nottinghamshire

www.brendawhite.co.uk

Shropshire

www.mansionsofthesoul.co.uk

Somerset

www.anexchangeoflove.com

South Yorkshire
www.uncommon-practice.org.uk
Suffolk
www.edgehypno.com/page001.html
www.animalhealer.co.uk
Warwickshire
www.allareonetherapies.co.uk
West Midlands
www.NDHypnotherapy.com
www.litehouse.info
www.auroratherapycentre.com
Wiltshire
www.livespastandpresent.co.uk.
Worcestershire
www.thetahealing-worcester.co.uk
www.regressionacademy.com/past-life-regression-
therapists.htm

NORTHERN IRELAND
www.hypnotherapistuk.com

SCOTLAND
www.wightrelax.co.uk
www.takurei.com
www.pastliferegression.co.uk

www.hypnotherapy-aberdeen.com
www.karmafix.co.uk

IRELAND

www.cottageretreat.net

WALES

www.hypnotherapy-regression.co.uk
www.sw-hypnosis.co.uk
www.regress.me.uk
www.previouslife.co.uk

AUSTRALIA

www.thefutureis.com
www.spiritualregression.com.au
www.themetaphysician.com.au

AUSTRIA

www.spiritualregression.de

CANADA

www.mindmeldconsulting.com
www.hypnotherapytoronto.com
www.lifebetweenlives.ca
www.ontariohypnosiscentre.com

CHINA
www.earth-association.org

GERMANY
www.esopsych.de
www.lifeconcepts.de
www.reiki-zentrum-dresden.de
www.bucolo-trappen.de

HONG KONG
www.pastnfuture.com

INDIA
www.theparnasala.com
www.acceleratedhealing.co.uk

ITALY
www.qion.it

MEXICO
www.alternativamexico.com

NETHERLANDS

www.pastlifetherapy.eu

www.iparrt.nl

www.wholeself.info

PERU

www.iarrt.org/members/profmembers.html#SouthAmerica

RUSSIA

pastlife.tsk.ru

SEYCHELLES

www.transform-therapies.sc

SLOVENIA

www.christian-reincarnation.com

SOUTH AFRICA

www.soulconnection.co.za

www.inspire-network.com

SPAIN

www.mariagemma.com

SWEDEN
www.sseah.se
www.regression.nu

TURKEY
www.radianced.com

USA
Arizona
www.tranquiltransitions.org
www.gen-assist.com
www.experienceSacredHealing.com
California
www.insightsfromwithin.com
Colorado
www.gregmchugh.com
Connecticut
www.soul2soulangelichealing.com
Florida
www.OneWorldMovement.org
Maryland
www.soundbalance.net
Massachusetts
www.yourinfinitequest.com

Minnesota

www.soundmindbodyhealing.com

Missouri

www.hypnosismo.com

Nebraska

www.XPHypnosis.com

Nevada

www.drtish.org

New Jersey

www.healinghypnotherapy.net

New Mexico

www.iarrt.org/members/profmembers.html#NM

www.nmhypnosis.com

New York

www.soulcenteredtherapy.com

North Dakota

www.chandaparkinson.com

Pennsylvania

www.auriclights.net

South Carolina

www.charlestonhypnotherapy.com

Texas

www.dallashypnosisconsultants.com

www.pastlifetherapy.org

Vermont
www.creativeeft.com
Virginia
www.hypnosoul.net
Washington
www.AwarenessEngineering.com
Wisconsin
www.hypnosisinwisconsin.com
www.shamanic-shift.org

Notes

Notes

Notes

About the Author

Based in beautiful Somerset, in the UK, and happily married for 40 years, Jenny Smedley, DPLT, is a qualified past-life regressionist, author, TV and radio presenter and guest, international columnist and spiritual consultant, specializing in the subjects of past lives and angels. She's also an animal intuitive and tree communicator.

Her own current life was turned around by a vision from one of her past lives, and problems and issues related to that life were healed and resolved in a few seconds.

Jenny has appeared on many TV shows and hundreds of radio shows, in countries including in the UK, USA, Australia, New Zealand, Iceland, Tasmania, the Caribbean, South Africa and Spain.

After being shown her Master Path by an angel, Jenny was given the ability to create Mirror Angel Portraits and remote-aura pictures, and to help others connect to their angels. Her website is www.jennysmedley.com.

© Tony Smedley

Hay House Titles of Related Interest